Long-Whiskers at play

LONG - WHISKERS

and the

TWO-LEGGED GODDESS

or

the true story of a "most objectionable" Nazi" and . . . half-a-dozen Cats

by

Savitri Devi

Long-Whiskers and the Two-Legged Goddess,
or The True Story of a
"Most Objectionable Nazi"
and... half-a-dozen Cats

By Savitri Devi

Revisionist Books
http://revisionistbooks.blogspot.com

ISBN 978-1-291-38858-9

CONTENTS

To U.G.

*the young comrade who used to come
to the little house in the woods*

FOREWORD.

Every person and every animal in this story has actually lived or is still alive-only their names, when at all mentioned, have been altered for obvious reasons. And this is precisely why this is neither a proper "cat story" in the usual sense of the word nor a bare psychological study of human "fanaticism," but both.

True life is never as simple as alleged portraits of it. And here, we have an instance of the fundamental complexity even of that psychology often considered as the simplest of all, namely, of that of a one-pointed political "fanatic," nay, of a militant upholder of an Ideology "of arrogance and violence" (to use the language of its enemies). Not only does the Doctrine itself, to which the heroine of this story is unconditionally devoted, appear greatly exceed mere "politics," when examined with the care it deserves, but the woman's devotion as a fact,-as an experience has unexpected roots :-roots in a whole world of values which one is not used to identify with her ideology.

In other words, our heroine's outlook seems somewhat different from that of many of those whom she would, herself, love and respect as her brothers in faith, because her approach to National Socialism is first and foremost aesthetic while theirs is mainly social and political. She sees it and lives it differently, because she is, whether she cares to admit it or not, different from most, or at least from many, of her comrades, even if she be as "fanatic" -as one-pointed; as uncompromising-as any of them. Fundamentally, she is in love with the beauty of life, which she beholds, unmarred, in animals, and more specially in felines; which she would like to behold in man also, but simply cannot-for man is not something complete, something "achieved," but a creature "on its way" to something higher, when not an irretrievably fallen creature in the process of decay. Our heroine therefore cannot love humanity-not even Aryan humanity. She cannot love it, for it is not uniformly beautiful, both in physical features and character. At most, she can and does love the creature of glory, which the natural elite of her race is aspiring, -tending-to become (or rebecome) : Aryan man in his perfection. It is not the preoccupation of living men's happiness-not the knowledge of her comrades' efficiency on the social plane-that brought her to her particular faith, but the dream-like vision of those Aryan supermen " as beautiful on their level, as the four-legged kings of the jungle on theirs,"[1] which the elite of her race could become, under its influence. In other words, she is a National Socialist because she beholds, in Adolf Hitler's teaching, "the one political doctrine infinitely more than political" -the only one founded upon the basic laws of Life-and the one Way of life that can lead the natural elite of mankind to its natural fulfilment in the state of supermanhood.

For the more and more numerous millions of increasingly mongrelised human beings, lost for the cause of collective supermanhood, our heroine has no time. She despises them profoundly, and comes in touch with them only when she cannot do otherwise: either to defend some animal (or animals in general) against them, or against some of them; or to fight them, whenever necessary; or to use them, whenever possible, for the benefit of the Aryan cause.

The "cat story" in which she is involved from the beginning goes at least to show that her eminently aesthetic approach to the alleged Ideology "of arrogance and violence" is possible, even logical-in perfect keeping, at any rate, with that which a French opponent[2] of the National Socialist doctrine once called its "appalling logic ". And this precisely because true Aryan racialism, National Socialism, to repeat its historic name,-not only is not a man-centred creed, but definitely excludes any man-centered outlook.

For this very reason, this book is anything but National Socialist propaganda: most people, nearly all people nowadays, have a man-centred outlook; to tell them bluntly how life-centred a great militant faith really is, is rather to turn them against it. To those few, however, who, far from looking upon man as the source of all values and the measure of all things, merely see in him, as Friedrich Nietzsche did, "a bridge between animalhood and supermanhood" our story might suggest the widely unpopular but, to us, quite obvious truth, that any beautiful, innocent beast -a finished handiwork of Nature, perfect on its own level-is decidedly more valuable than a human specimen that does not (or, by birth, cannot) tend towards the one thing that justifies, if at all, the existence of man: the perfection of superman; more valuable, we say, because, be it of limited scope, a finished-flawless-work of art is always better than a failure. Those might well be attracted to our heroine's aristocratic faith, and come to it, contrarily to many of its former supporters, fully aware of its remotest implications, and therefore fully knowing what they are doing; come to it and never turn back. They would be welcome: the militant minority needs those to whom its "appalling logic" appeals without reservations. Yet, we repeat: this is not, cannot be, propaganda. For who cares for minorities in the present world . Minorities do not count; they are not dangerous -or not supposed to be.

1. See "Gold In the Furnace" (Calcutta edition 1952 P. 210) and "The Lightning and the Sun," Calcutta edition 1958; Chapter XV : "Gods on Earth -by Savitri Devi.
2. Mr. R. Grassot, of the French Information Bureau, in Baden-Baden in 1948.

PART I

BLACK-AND-WHITE

CHAPTER I

THE CALL IN THE NIGHT.

This happened in one of the innumerable by-lanes of immense Calcutta, on a beautiful, warm starry night' during the Second World War...A soft, subdued call of love and of distress broke the silence at regular intervals: " Rrmiaou; rrmiaou;... rrrrmia-ou '"

One of the many half-starving mother-cats that existed on the refuse-heaps of the narrow, dirty lane, knew that her kitten was **somewhere** near-by-very near-but she could neither see it nor get at it. In fact, she knew where it was : there, behind that high wooden wall, that stood, impenetrable, in front of her. And she knew that it wanted to come to her; that it was hungry,-poor baby-cat ! And although she hardly had any milk-for she was herself but skin and bone-she wanted to feed it. It was calling her answering her smothered mews with desperate, high-pitched shrieks, as loud as its tiny young throat could cry: "meeou ! meeou ! meeou ! "

But the forbidding wall-the double doors of a "go-down "-stood between the little creature and her. For the thousandth time, she walked to and fro, to and fro, along the stone edge that ran at the foot of the " wall ", in other words, the first step that led into the go-down. And for the thousandth time she mewed and mewed-and tried to find a crack, a hole, an opening of some sort between the ill fitting planks; some means of reaching her baby-cat. And for thousandth time the baby-cat mewed back in its turn, in high-pitched calls of despair: "meeou! meeou! meeou,"

As long as there were cars and buses, and tramways and bullock-carts continuously going up and down the near-by bustling Dharmatala Street, and rick-shaws and bicycles going up and down the lane, and open-air sellers shouting or customers at the corner of both, the mother-cat's voice, and even that of the kitten, was drowned in the general noise. Nobody could hear it, save, of course, the people who stood just before the closed go-down. But these busied themselves with their own affairs, as thou heard nothing; for they did not care. As the traffic grew lesser and lesser, even in the main street, and as the lane gradually became empty and quiet, the mews of distress became more and more audible. Yet nobody seemed to pay the slightest attention: one after the other, the people who dwelt in the lane closed their shutters and went to bed. Millions of stars now appeared in the deep, dark immensity above; millions of suns, each one with its satellites whirling round it, at God alone knows how many thousand light-years distance from this tiny Earth; all going their way, in mathematical harmony.

But upon this insignificant Earth, a speck of dust in fathomless infinity, out of the gutter in that obscure lane in Calcutta, the mew of the poor emaciated mother-cat calling her kitten, and the cry of the poor kitten calling its mother, rent the divine silence of space, again and again and again, without end. How many other cries of distress or cries of pain rent it from other places in that self-same city ? How many, from other places on earth ? How many, from other worlds, where living creatures struggle and suffer ?

Then, at last, all of a sudden, somewhat far away, a tall white form stepped forth on to a balcony of one of the houses of the main street, the back-windows of which overlooked the lane from a distance. It remained there for a while, and disappeared,-only to be seen again, five minutes later, walking up the lane. It was that of a fair woman wrapped in a **sari**; of a lover of dumb creatures, and especially of felines, who had never seen or heard an animal in need of help without doing all she could for it. Guided by the sound of the kitten's cries, the woman went straight to the closed go-down.

CHAPTER II

HELIODORA.

She had come years before from far-away Europe, for reasons of her own,-reasons entirely different from those for which other foreigners settle in India. One of the things that had attracted her to the hallowed Land was the fact that, contrary to the Christians, Mohammedans and Jews, the Hindus neither acknowledge an unbreachable gap between " man" and the rest of living creatures nor believe that those creatures have been brought into being **for** man. She had-logically, yet erroneously,-drawn the conclusion that such people must necessarily be kind to animals in practical life; kinder, at any rate, than those who process a faith or a philosophy centred around the "infinite value of human life" alone. Another reason why she had come was that India is the only land on earth in which Aryan Gods,-akin to those Europe used to adore, before Christianity was forced upon her people-are still worshipped, and Aryan principles, inherited from the fair invaders of six thousand years ago[1], accepted without discussion; the only land, for example, in which the bulk of the population has never ceased believing in the God-ordained hierarchy of human races.

These two aspects of her psychology sprang in reality from one and the same source, namely from the woman's essentially aesthetic outlook on life. She maintained that a beautiful healthy animal, in fact, a beautiful healthy tree, is infinitely more precious than a sickly human being, **a fortiori** than a cripple or otherwise deficient man, woman or child. And she held the Aryan race, to which she was proud to belong, to be the finest race on earth, and all that which exalts it and its natural values to be good, mainly because the Aryan type of human being is-or was, in her eyes, at least-**the** most beautiful of all.

And, having read that a certain Greek named Heliodorus -an envoy at the court of an Indian king of the fourth century before the Christian era,-had once, somewhere near Bhilsa, set up a stele upon which he described himself as a "worshipper of Vishnu," she had taken the name of Heliodora. She too was an Aryan of the West who had been drawn to Indian ways, out of the feeling that they were **not strange** to her; that they were the ways of Aryan people who adapted themselves to a tropical environment and to life in the midst of a numerically overwhelming foreign population of many races. Apart from that, the name suited her, for she was a devout Sun-worshipper.[2] For years she had been living under that name. Nobody knew what she had, originally, been called.

*   *   *

She was seated-cross-legged, in the Oriental manner, upon a mattress upon which was spread one of those mats, made in Shylet, which are as fine as cloth; and she was writing. A smooth plank, which lay upon her lap, served the purpose of a writing-table. And there were cats, some ten or twelve of them, or more, lying here and there, all over the place, some upon the mat, some upon the bulky cushions that lay in a row against the wall, others upon the cool, shiny floor, of dark-red, artificial marble. One beautiful, half-angora tom-cat, all black save for a hardly visible white spot upon his breast, had stretched himself his whole length upon the papers at Heliodora's side, softly purring. This was Sadhu, her favourite cat,-her favourite because the most beautiful of all, among those she had. The only piece of furniture in the white-washed room was a book-case full of books; the only decoration in it, an enormous brass plate, entirely inlaid with red enamel, of Jaipur workmanship, which stood against the wall upon that book-case. In front of that plate could be seen, within a frame, an enlarged photograph of Adolf Hitler feeding a young deer-one of the loveliest pictures of the German Leader. Heliodora was not a German. Nor had she ever seen the Maker of the Third Reich. But she was, partly at least, of Nordic blood, and hailed in him the Saviour of her race, the Friend of creatures, and the exponent of everlasting Wisdom. And she worshipped him. Fresh pink lotuses lay in a round, fiat, painted earthen vessel, at

16

century before the Christian era,-had once, somewhere near the foot of the picture, and three sticks of incense were smoking before it, fixed in the holes at the top of a brass burner, which had the shape of the sacred sign "Aum": Heliodoia's tribute of love to her Leader; and the first-fruits of that of the whole of Eastern Aryandom, which she had come to conquer for him.

The woman stopped writing, and started thinking about the war.

In later, darkening days, how often was she to look back to this glorious early spring of 1942, in which one had experienced, to the full, the thrill of victory, and joyous confidence in the destiny of the world ! Now, she was living that stage of unmixed optimism. And did not events seem to justify her feelings as well as those of the millions of people who, like herself,-although, perhaps, from a standpoint somewhat different from hers-firmly believed in Hitler's mission ? Indeed, on all fronts, the situation was -or seemed to be-splendid. The German army was successfully standing the Russian winter; and Stalin was calling for help-for arms and ammunitions-from his western allies; Rommel was advancing along the Libyan coast towards the Egyptian border, and would, apparently, not take long to reach Alexandria and Port-Said, and to hinder England's normal communications with India; in the East, Germany's allies, the Japanese, had taken Singapur only a few days before-on the eleventh of February, exactly two thousand and a hundred and two years after the foundation of the Empire of the Rising Sun, according to officially accepted Tradition, undoubtedly a good omen-and they were now rapidly conquering Burma; and they would conquer Assam and East Bengal and Calcutta, and march to Delhi,-where the irresistible German Army, pushing on from Russia through High Asia and the historic Khyber Pass, would no doubt meet them. There was only one thing that depressed Heliodora in all that, and this was the fact that, being in Calcutta, she had personally witnessed none of the parades of victory, specially not the one along the Avenue Des Champs Elysees, in conquered Paris, on the 14th of June 1940. She could not forgive herself for not having gone back to Europe before the war, when it was yet time. She cursed her fate, for not having been able to go in 1939, when she **had** tried so

17

hard then, managed to leave India, she would have been sending messages on the Berlin wireless in modern Greek, in Bengali, and perhaps one or two more other languages for which there were few applicants. **That** would have been a job for her ! And sooner or later someone would have had the good sense of introducing her to the Fuhrer; she felt quite positive about that. She would have seen "him": heard "him", speak; speak **to her**, personally ! "Alas " thought she. Still, all would be well if the Germans and the Japanese were soon to meet in imperial Delhi. Then "he" would come there and receive the allegiance of the East as well as of the West. And she would go and greet him.

Just as she was thinking of this, Sadhu, who had, up till then, been lying upon her papers, stretched himself and turned towards her his round black, glossy head, with golden eyes.

"My fury beauty; my black tiger ! " said she, as she stroked him under his chin, in answer to his blissful glance:

"My black tiger with one tiny white spot-only one ! "

The reply was a soft, regular purr.

An unexpected thought crossed Heliodora's mind, like a flash of lightning: "Had I gone to Europe in 1939, or even in 1940, I should not have had this lovely creature, nor, in fact, any of these cats to which I have given a home. They probably all would have been dead, by now-would have Died of misery, in some gutter, without love, poor beautiful felines "' And a strange question followed that thought: " Was it **for them** that I was fated to remain here ?"

She knew the thought was a nonsensical one and the question too. For of what account was the life and happiness of any creatures, nay, of any human beings , including her own, compared with the service of the Aryan Reich and of the Cause of truth ? But then she remembered a lovely sentence, which she herself had quoted number of times in the meetings she used to address; a sentence that could have been written by a Hindu, but which was in fact taken from Alfred Rosenberg's booklet commonly described as the " Nazi Catechism ": "Behold Godhead in every living creature, animal and plant"- in other words: worship everlasting Life in all sentient beings.

" How near we are to Hinduism ! " thought she, for the millionth time. "Our principles are exactly the same: the self-same Aryan principles that were those of Northern Europe, before it fell a prey to Christianity." And for the millionth time, she dreamed of making that identity manifest in the eyes both of the Hindus and of the Germans and other racially conscious Aryans of the West, and of giving Adolf Hitler the reverence and active support of the whole of Indo-European humanity, re-awakened to the pride of its own eternal values.

*   *   *

Sadhu got up, stepped into the woman's lap, and there, curled himself into a ball, with his head up-side-down and a front-paw stretched out, in one of those graceful and unexpected positions which cats are so fond of taking. Heliodora could never get a tangible mark of confidence from any of her cats,-or, by the way, from any beast, without feeling deeply touched; and also without recalling in her mind, and detesting, the thousands of human beings who betray such confidence, every-day in some way or another. Presently, she took the soft velvet paw, whose sharp, curved claws were drawn in, in both her hands, and stroked it. The claws slowly came out, and then again disappeared into their sheathes. And a louder purr, that one could feel through the cat's thick, warm coat, specially at the level of the neck, was again the pet's answer.

Heliodora felt happy,-half reconciled to the fact that she had not seen the victory parades in Europe, in " glorious '40' ", "Anyhow, there soon will be more such victory parades to be seen here in Asia," thought she. "In the meantime, had I succeeded in going to Europe a year and a half ago, where would you all be, you happy furry ones ? And where would be the dogs that wait every evening at the corner of the lane for me to bring them something to eat ? 'Behold Godhead in every living creature, animal or plant.' It is better to live up to that spirit, which is **ours**, and whose victory in the world would be our victory, than to watch military parades."

But it suddenly seemed to her as though she had heard a mew of distress coming from somewhere far away in the narrow lake. She quickly went and opened the window wide (she had shut it, as usual, to keep out the sound of the neighbouring radios, and that of people jabbering on the near-by terrace). Immediately, the mews of distress seemed to her alarmingly high-pitched. But where could they come from ? She stood on the balcony and listened. The mews were, quite definitely, coming from the lane. Heliodora, who had never heard an animal cry without finding out what the matter was and then trying her best **to do something** about it, threw a shawl over her shoulders, took a jug of milk in one hand, a saucer-and her house keys-in the other, and went down-stairs.

Two or three minutes later, she was in the dark lane, in front of the place from which the mews were coming.

1. See Lekomanya Tilak's books "Orion" and "The Arctic Home or the Vedas"

This was Sadhu, her favourite cat

CHAPTER III

THE BLISSFUL HOME.

The mother-cat ran away at the woman's approach. She had experienced nothing but cruelty from the two-legged sort: they had thrown stones, or water (generally cold, but, on one occasion, boiling water) at her, or tried to hit her with a stick whenever hunger had driven her into one of their houses. How could she know that there were some kind ones among them ? She ran away; then walked a few steps back; once more called her lost kitten, and ran away again as she saw Heliodora's figure before the go-down. The woman poured a little milk into her saucer, put it down on the ground, some ten yards away, and went back to examine the door: to see whether she could not find a crack that could be made larger, a loose plank, that could be pulled away-some means by which she could free the kitten. She called the mother-cat from a distance: "Puss, puss, puss ..." and waited, without moving at all.

The mother-cat was torn between hunger and fear. Hunger won, and Heliodora saw her cautiously walk back-for the third time-and put her mouth into the good milk and start lapping it. She still remained completely immobile. The mother-cat looked up, saw there was no danger, and continued lapping. Heliodora had discovered in the door a plank that looked loose. But she did not-yet-proceed to pull it out. "Let the cat finish her milk," thought she: " the kitten can wait; it cannot run away anyhow"

As she saw the saucer was empty, she went and refilled it. The cat again fled at her approach, but returned as soon as she had walked back to the go-down. And again she lapped the milk greedily. It was indeed a pleasure to get two saucers of milk when one had eaten nothing the whole day but a few corns of rice gathered from the dust-heaps, among kitchen ashes and rotting, foul-smelling vegetable-refuse ! And for the first time in her miserable lie, such a pleasure was directly associated with the presence of one of "them"-one of the frightful Two-legged ones. She did not know what to make of it. Nor what to do: remain, or run away. The baby-cat was still calling her; and that tall, big creature that had brought the milk, did not look as though it would try to hit her, or throw water at her. So she remained... but at a prudent distance : with Two-legged ones, one is never sure.

*   *   *

Heliodora had caught hold of the loose plank, and was jerking at it, trying to pull it out. Now and then, she held her breath, listened whether anyone was coming, or whether the people who lived opposite the go-down were opening their shutters to shout at her. It would surely not have been the first time she would have had a row with human beings on account of her sense of duty towards other creatures. She was accustomed to such incidents and fully prepared to face them. But this time, no such thing happened And after a few jerks, the plank came out while the woman, losing hold of it, fell backwards, flat upon the ground in the middle of the lane. Her first thought, as she pulled herself together, was: "What a good thing that I ad put down my milk jug ! Had that fallen over, I should have had to go and fetch more milk, and in the meantime both cat and kitten would have run away. Now, the poor creatures will have a home."

She poured a little more milk into the saucer, and laid the latter **inside** the go-down, at the new entrance which she had just opened. She kept her hand, absolutely immobile, above the saucer, and waited. The kitten, which she could not see, for it was pitch-dark, soon came. She heard it lapping the milk. Then, suddenly letting down her hand, she caught hold of the little creature as firmly as she could, though without hurting it. But the baby-cat, that was thoroughly afraid of "two-legged beasts"-for its mother had, in a mysterious way, warned it against the nasty tricks they can play upon one-defended itself heroically: it spat and scratched, and bit deeply into the woman's finger. Heliodora admired the pluck of that tiny fluffy living ball, which she now held in both hands, and she stroked its fur with infinite love, and laid a kiss upon its silky round head-the first human kiss the baby-cat had ever received. The little creature was at once convinced that **this** was not a "two-legged beast" like most of them, but a real friend and protector of the feline race. Through the enchantment of loving caresses, this fact imposed itself, in all its overwhelming forcefulness, upon the kitten's consciousness. And the reaction was sudden and complete; unbelievable to anyone who is not well acquainted with feline nature: a loud purr answered the woman's touch, as the kitten curled himself up in her left hand, while she continued stroking him with her right one. The baby-cat was totally conquered: already sure this huge two-legged creature loved him, and ready to believe in human kindness.

Heliodora looked backwards to see what the mother-cat was doing. She saw her step into the go-down and out again; she heard her mew-that same soft, subdued mew of yearning and of distress which sounded to her even more pathetic than before, now that she knew the poor beast would not find her little one. For a few seconds, she had half a mind to put the kitten down, so that his mother might carry him away. But then, as she felt the thin furry body, purring in her hand, and as she thought of the miserable life of the average Calcutta cat-one could say: of the average street cat in the East, nay, already in southern Europe,- she hesitated to do so. She stooped down, however, and, after refilling her saucer with milk for the third time, waited. She would show the kitten to his mother. Perhaps the mother would follow him, in spite of all, to his new home; who knows ?

The mother-cat drank the third saucer of milk: she was hungry. Heliodora did not move, but called her from the place where she had halted: " Puss, puss, puss "' And, just at that moment, the kitten, who had stretched himself upon her arm, stood up and mewed. This was not the high-pitched cry of distress that his tiny throat had been thrusting out for God alone knows how many hours, but a bold mew of satisfaction between two purrs. And the mother-cat heard it, and answered it: "Rrmiaou ! rrrmiaou !" Now she knew where her kitten was. And she was beginning to feel that he was not in wicked hands. His mew was a happy one. Moreover, **that** two-legged creature was not like the others: it did not chase one away; it gave one milk, and allowed one to drink it in peace, remaining at a reasonable distance. Again the mother-cat looked up at her baby, and mewed. Heliodora spoke to her softly. Come, my cat ! Come, my pretty one ! Puss, puss, puss... " And she slowly walked back home, looking round now and then.

The mother-cat was following her all right; following her own kitten, with those same subdued mews. The mews went straight to the woman's heart. It seemed to her as though they were now addressed to her and meant: "Do give me back my little one ! It is all I have in the world; all I love !" Again she was tempted to put the kitten down. But again it was clear to her that this would be thrusting him back into the untold misery of street-life in Calcutta, **along with** his mother. And she wanted to save both, if she could.

She soon reached the door leading into her stair-case. Would the grown-up cat follow her **into** the house ? She stepped in and looked around. The cat was there, a few steps away, gazing at her as though wishing to say 'Why won't you give me back my kitten-my only one? " and mewing once more, calling the little creature for the last time. Heliodora felt the cat's distress as though it had been her own. "Poor beast !" thought she, "Am I to take away all she loves ?. But if only she would come in I should keep them both. They are twelve already; they'd be fourteen "

And she put down the kitten and waited. The mother-cat still outdoors, called for the thousandth time: "Rrmiaou ! Rrrmiaou !" The baby-cat took to running towards her, and she towards him. Heliodora, who was watching the minute she would cross the threshold, suddenly closed the door, and caught both cat and kitten under the hanging end of her " sari ". And paying no heed to the animal's struggle to free itself- the scratches of the outstretched claws and the loud shrieks of terror-she hurried upstairs to the second floor, put down her Jug (now empty) and her saucer, opened the door and slammed it shut as soon as she had stepped in. Then, she loosened her embrace. The cat sprang onto the floor of the room that was henceforth to be her home, and ran and hid herself under the book-case. Heliodora, still holding the kitten upon her arm, went into the kitchen and came back with a plate full of rice mixed with bits of fish, which she laid upon the floor. **Then**

26

she let the kitten go, and from a distance, she watched him eat-and then finish the milk that was still lying at the bottom of the many cats' large shallow plate. The mother-cat had not moved: she was no longer hungry enough to overcome her fear.

*   *   *

For two or three days she would not come out from her hiding-place, save to eat-and that, only when the "two-legged one" was not to be seen. She would growl and spit at the other cats. And she even scratched Sadhu for having dared come too near her, be it in the most friendly mood -apparently, to rub his splendid, round glossy head against hers. Her kitten was the only one she wanted. She continued calling him in the same loving voice, with the same mews of tenderness: "Rrmiaou !, Rrrrmiaou !" And she licked him as he lay hanging at her breast, purring thrusting his little paws into her fur.

But as time passed, things changed. First of all, the mother-cat's body took shape: her neck no longer looked skinny; her bones no longer jutted out; her coat became shiny. And she had more milk. And she gradually became accustomed to the house and to the other cats. As for the kitten, he was growing into a fat, fluffy ball of fur, happy and playful, and full of affection for Heliodora, in whose lap he lay-alone or **with** his mother-when he was not amusing himself with Sadhu's brushy tail, or trying to catch flies, or jumping at his own shadow on the wall.

He was an ordinary black and white kitten, rather black than white,-the cross-breed of his mother, who was all white, save for a black patch on her head, another on he back, and another on the tip of her tail, and of a tom-cat as black as night-and particularly well marked. He had a broad, round head, short, velvety ears, large, transparent green eyes that glowed against their background of black fur. Only his nose, chin, belly and front paws were white. The paws were broad in proportion to the body, as those of a strong young tom-cat should be. The whiskers were stiff and long enough to be the pride of any conceited feline. But this beautiful kitten was not conceited. He had no idea how beautiful he was. He was all love and playfulness, nothing more. Yet Heliodora, who generally did not give names to her cats (" Sadhu " already had his name when Zobeida, his first mistress, too poor to feed him properly, had handed him over to the " cat **mem-sahib** ") often called him " Long-whiskers "

He was now lying in the woman's lap, sucking his mother, stamping his front-paws in turn into her warm fur, and purring. The mother, completely relaxed, was also purring-a soft, regular purr of unmarred bliss. The other cats were dozing here and there: some upon the mattress where Heliodoia was sitting, some upon the cushions, some upon the floor. Sadhu, who had been sleeping in the sunshine for quite a long time, suddenly decided that it was too hot, and went and stretched himself in a cool shady comer. Just one sunray, coming in through a crack in the shutters of the near-by window, still fell directly upon him, and made it clear that his coat, that one generally would have called "black," was not really so, but dark, very dark brown. The tips of the soft silky hairs even appeared light reddish-brown, wherever the golden ray touched them.

As carefully as she possibly could-so as not to disturb the cats in her lap,-Heliodora pulled the curtain across the other window, the shutters of which were open, put aside the newspaper that she had been reading, and leaned against the wall. She started stroking the two heaps of living fur-mother and kitten-that purred a little louder at the contact of her hands, and enjoyed the peace of her little room full of happy cats; also the peace of the verandah outside, full of healthy green plants, in the shade of which the cats often used to lie. The " Statesman "[1] slipped down from the cushion upon which she had laid it, onto the floor, where one of the cats took to tearing it up. Heliodoia smiled, and let him go on. "The paper can hardly be put to a better use" thought she.

It was, as always,-and as all newspapers were, in Allied-controlled countries-full of nothing but anti-Nazi Propaganda. And the propaganda was, as always, an appeal to the reader's "human feelings". Heliodora had no "human feelings" in the ordinary sense of the word. She had been, from her very childhood, much too profoundly shocked at the behaviour of man towards animals in particular and living Nature in general, to have any sympathy for people suffering on account

28

of their being Jews or friends of the Jews. The Jews were after all responsible for that silly exaltation of " man "-regardless of race and personality-above all creatures; for that criminal denial of the sacred unity of Life and of the laws of Life, in the name of man's special value and so-called "dignity". Heliodora recalled in her mind the threefold classification of beings according to the Kabbala : the "uncreated One, who creates," i.e. God; the "created one who creates"-man; and finally, the "created beings that So not create"-the rest of whatever exists : animals, plants, minerals. "What nonsense '" thought she. "As if all human beings were capable of creation ! Only a very small minority of them are. Then, why exalt "all men" instead of "all creatures" 'To infuse into them-even into the naturally better ones-the contempt of race and personality, so that the ugly Jew may alone control the mass of nondescript cross-breeds that will, in course of time, be the tangible outcome of that unnatural contempt ?"

In addition to that, the fact that the Jews are expected to eat the flesh of those animals only that have been slaughtered in that most cruel manner prescribed by their religion, was in Heliodora's eyes, the worst of all. Any slaughter-houses were an abomination to her; but "kosher" ones !-no treatment was bad enough when meted out to people who upheld or tolerated such institutions !

And that is why the propaganda,-written for the average " decent people ", i.e., for the average flesh-eaters, who have accepted the Christian, in other words, the Jewish, scale values, as the basis of their outlook on life and subsequently of their ethics-had upon Heliodora exactly the contrary effect from that which its promoters had aimed at obtaining. It invariably gave her new reasons to feel proud of being a National Socialist, and to want the destruction of that so-called "civilisation,"-that dull plutocracy-for the love of which one was repeatedly told to "fight Nazism". In this paper that sharp teeth and claws were just now tearing to bits, for sheer delight, was an article about so-called "Nazi atrocities". Vivisection had been abolished in the Third Reich, admitted the author of that article, but... " only to be replaced by experimentation upon human beings," namely, upon anti-Nazis-specially Jews, but sometimes also particularly pro-Jewish people of other stocks-" taken among the inmates of the concentration camps." Heliodora, who had always looked upon experimentation upon unconcerned beasts neither "for" nor "against" any cause-as the vilest of all crimes, and **wanted** dangerous human beings to be used in their stead, if such research work **had** to be done, simply thought: "I wish this **is** true, and not just a propaganda tale ! If it is true, it is perhaps the best thing the grand Third Reich has done under the inspiration of its god-like Leader-all praise to him '" And she again stroked the mother-cat and kitten, now both asleep in her lap. A light purr answered her touch, and a faint ripple ran along the two soft, furry bodies. Heliodora, whom the newspaper article she had just read had deeply impressed, and who was gifted with a vivid power of imagination, thought of experiments performed upon such lovely creatures as those lying in her lap around her. And she shuddered.

She recalled an episode from the days she had been a student, some years before, in a French university.

She had once entered a certain room-by mistake. A door led from there into several other rooms, communicating with one another, one at least of which was a vivisection chamber. And in front of that door, tied to the handle of it by a leash, had stood a dog-an ordinary light-brown dog, as thousands of others one can meet in the streets, all over the world. And that dog had stood up upon his hind legs and pulled upon his leash and tried to reach Heliodora as she had entered, feeling, no doubt, that she was a friend of creatures, and wanting her to stroke his head. Heliodora had known, even before asking anybody and getting a confirmation of her horrible intuition, that that dog was to be vivisected. She had not been able to bring herself to stroke it: any such caress had appeared to her as an act of treason: a promise of human kindness to that trusting beast, that was about to experience in its own body one of the most revolting forms of human cruelty; a dirty lie. Had nobody been there, she would have untied the dog, taken it away, saved it anyhow and at any cost. But there had been several people there. There had been nothing she could have done or even said, with any hope of drawing that living creature-one among millions -away from its atrocious fate.

Nothing ! She had looked at the dog, and tears had filled her eyes, and a cold sensation of horror had run along her spine, and wild hatred towards mankind,-lucid, relentless, patient, immortal hatred for the whole species, save the hallowed minority who shared her feelings; hatred that she had always known, always experienced, only somewhat less intensely, and that would never slacken, never lessen, never change, in this life and all her lives to come,-had filled her breast. Knowing that all words would be lost upon the men sitting in that room, still she had not been able to leave without a sentence : a condemnation to death ; a curse : " A civilisation that takes experiments upon dumb creatures as a matter of course should be wiped out ! May I see it blown to pieces within my life-time ! " had she proclaimed, trembling with indignation as she had made for the door. The dog, pulling hard on his leash and stretching his neck, had managed to lick her hands. She now remembered how this episode had haunted her for weeks and weeks. And she felt relieved at the thought that, in the young, regenerated German Reich, round which, after the war, a new Europe would crystallize and take shape, such abominations no longer occurred. For the human beings who, according to the " Statesman ", were alleged to replace the four-legged mammals in the "service of science," she had no pity. First, even if not necessarily Jews, they were anti-Nazis, enemies of all she loved; so it served them right. And second, even if they all were not; even if there existed among them a few non-political people, interned by mistake (mistakes will happen in war time), it mattered little: non-political people are generally admirers of " Science " with a capital S; they call Pasteur, that torturer of hundreds of beasts, a " great man, " and look up to other such criminals as " benefactors of mankind "; not one of them in a million had fought all his life, as she had, against vivisection and other such crimes against Life, let alone against man-centred religions and philosophies. So, let them suffer and die for that which they admired and loved ! (She was prepared to suffer and die for what she loved and admired: for the great new Aryan Reich, with its proud **life**-centred doctrine that set a beautiful healthy cat or dog far above a dangerous or deficient human being of any race). She also remembered that the person at the head of the " Physiology research department " in that university where she had been a chemistry student, was a Jewess. Where would she now be ?-that one under whose supervision live dogs' skulls were taken off, and experiments performed upon the animals' raw brains ? In some camp in Germany, by this time -she hoped. Waiting to be gassed, or perhaps at this very minute in a gas-chamber. And Heliodora thought, with a smile of satisfaction : " For once: 'the right person in the right place ! '"

And she continued stroking the soft, warm, furry bodies that lay peacefully in her lap, purring themselves to sleep.

*   *   *

This went on day after day: food-lovely food: rice mixed with fish (the only trouble was that the bits of fish were so finely mashed up with the rice that one could hardly pick them out separately, however much one tried) and milk: creamy milk that Long-whiskers and his mother had never had an opportunity of tasting before that night in front of the go-down;-blissful sleep, never more interrupted by a hard kick, or a stone, or water, thrown no one knew from where upon one's back; and that soft, regular stroking of one's fur by a magical hand, that sent one into the cats' seventh Heaven; a magical hand that seemed to know all the subtleties of a cat's nature, and never stroked one when one wanted to be left alone. And that deep, comfortable lap, into which one could jump whenever one liked and where one could remain-asleep or awake-as long as one pleased; to which one was never brought by force, and from which one was never turned away ! Security **and** freedom at the same time. What more could a cat -in fact, any feline-desire ?

So Long-whiskers grew into a splendid big tom-cat: twice as big as his mother (that had known a very hard life) and even bigger than Sadhu. And, which is more, even more beautiful than Sadhu, in spite of the latter's half angora fur. Long-whiskers had the short fur of the usual gutter-cat who has no angora blood at **all**. But that fur was extraordinarily thick, and as soft and glossy as the softest and glossiest plush. The black portions-by far the largest -shone in the sunshine, every individual hair having, if seen alone, a shimmer of rainbow shades about it. The white parts were as spotless as snow. The round head with its dreamy greenish-yellow eyes (rather green than yellow) had become broader, with bulging cheeks: tigerish. And the cat carried himself like a miniature tiger: his proud head erect or... stretched downwards, with the short, black, velvety ears thrown back and flattened, whenever he was watching a prey: a mouse or just a cockroach !-his supple body undulating as he placed his powerful paws one before the other, regularly.

Heliodora often gazed at him for a long time, feeling so happy that she had taken in the royal creature, when he had been but a miserable starving kitten, mewing desperately. Not that she considered that his evolution had in any way been **her** work. She knew it was Nature's doing. And there were thousands of starving kittens that she could never reach, the sufferings and death of which she could never hear of -and not only kittens, but puppies, calves, lambs, young horses and donkeys, all sorts of young creatures-that would grow into the loveliest specimens of their kind, were they only to receive the care and affection which Long-whiskers had enjoyed, or were they at least just left alone, with enough to eat every day. She could not help feeling, however, that she had worked " in the sense of Nature's finality ", and that was enough to make her happy. It was, it had always been her ambition to work-on human plane **and** in connection with all living things-in the direction pointed out by Nature; " in the spirit of Creation, " to express it in those very words of her beloved Fuehrer that she had quoted so many times.'2

And Long-whiskers knew he was loved and admired, and he was also happy. He would come and rub his silky head against Heliodora, look up to her as she stroked it, and jump upon her lap. Or, if the lap was " occupied "-by Sadhu, or maybe by one of the other cats, now more and more numerous,-he would snarl till the occupant would at last get down and let him have the place. He did not like his feline companions-save the she-cats, of course and especially not Sadhu. Nor did Sadhu like him:-the new-comer, the intruder who was getting so much of the love and care that he had once enjoyed alone, a long time before, when he had still been the only cat which Heliodora had.

At times, the woman, who did not want to hurt his feelings, would pick up Sadhu and hold him in her arms and stroke him, with the same words of love she had always used: " My velvet ! My purring fur ! My black tiger ! "

And the cat could not help purring indeed, in the magic embrace of that more-than-feline creature who loved him as much as ever. But then, as he would become aware of Long-whiskers' presence, he would suddenly struggle himself out of his mistress' arms, jump upon the floor and go and seat himself, with perfect feline dignity, in the remotest corner of the room-as far away as possible even from the other many cats. Then, nine times out of ten, Long-whiskers would give out a particularly soft mew, and, after this notice, spring upon Heliodora's shoulders and settle down in her arms-in Sadhu's place-if she was willing to have him. And she **was** willing ! Even if she was not-if she happened to have, at that moment, something else to do-she soon **became** willing. (How could one refuse the advances of that enormous, panther-like cat, Long-whiskers, wanting to be caressed ?) Admittedly, she felt sorry for poor Sadhu. But there was nothing she could do to reconcile the two felines, which she both loved.

Each one had his own beauty: the half-angora and the gutter tom-cat. In fact, all her cats-now some twenty or twenty-five of them: Long-whiskers' mother had had two more kittens, and Heliodora had brought in a few from the streets-were gutter-cats, except Sadhu. She sometimes thought of those people who spend a lot of money on pets with a pedigree, yet would do nothing to help a poor starving street-cat or dog lying at their door-step She despised such heartless snobs. " What pedigree have they themselves, anyhow ? " wondered she. " Half of them don't even know who their great-grandfathers were ! As for Eurasians and half-Jews who insist upon having only animals 'of good breed,' well... " The very idea disgusted her. Moreover, the Fuhrer had for all times to come condemned such unnatural hobbies and such a topsy-turvy world. One day, as she was precisely thinking of this, and recalling in her mind his words of wisdom,[3] Long-whiskers-who was lying flat upon the floor, for he was too hot-looked up to her and started purring... as though he had wanted to all with her belief that racial selection was a concern of the two-legged ones. But of course, it was a mere coincidence.

However it be, life was lovely in Heliodora's quiet home. It was not only the good food and the woman's caresses, and that complete freedom that the felines appreciated so much. It **was**... the atmosphere. The cats, in whose confused consciousness, all these things were blended together, could naturally not separate that from the rest. But had they been able to do so-and had they been in possession of human speech-they would have called it " restful " " serene ". Time did not " pass " in that blissful home; it **glided**. And one felt it glide-over play and sleep, meals, and dreamy relaxation at Heliodora's side or in her lap. One felt it glide as the invisible caress of some mysterious great Being, in whose care one was safe. The wide world outside seethed with all manner of struggle: struggle for food; struggle to remain out of the way of dogs, and of cruel children, who are worse, and occasionally, of grown-up two-legged creatures; struggle to keep the kittens out the reach of such enemies. Here, all was so peaceful and so easy. The cats that had but recently come in from the street, skin and bone, as Long-whiskers and his mother had once been, appreciated the difference. The broad verandah with its many green plants, in the shade of which one could doze or play, chase and catch an occasional beetle (or sometimes-at night-a mouse) was, for a long time at least, a sufficient field of adventure for them. Some of them, she-cats, for the most, never attempted to see the street again.

But Long-whiskers was now over a year and a half old. He had long forgotten his wretched babyhood: the pitiless struggle for mother's milk, in which his brother and two sisters had perished-died of starvation, one after the other-while he, the strongest of the litter, had survived, God alone knew how; and the fear of a crowd of horrible creatures, four-legged and two-legged, that barked or shouted, ran after one, threw stones or water at one, and sometimes caught hold of one by one's tail, or leg, or head. It had been a sheer miracle that he had always managed to bite and scratch himself out of their clutches, tiny as he had been then. So many poor street kittens had not been so lucky !

But that all lay far far away within the mist of the past. And tell her how fully he agreed with her philosophy, and above Long-whiskers had not the faintest recollection of it -save, perhaps somewhere very deep in his sub-conscious mind. All he was aware of was a confused but ardent longing to live exciting adventures, or what he dimly deemed to be such. Some elemental power within him was urging him to wander into the limitless world beyond Heliodora's peaceful room and beautiful verandah : down the winding iron stairs at the other end of what appeared to him as a shady " avenue, " into the court-yard that he had never seen but from above; into the street, which he did not remember. So, upon a moon-lit night, as the urge had grown overwhelming, he got up from the mat where he had been lying for an hour or more, softly stroked by Heliodora's loving hand. He sat for a while upon the window-sill, gazing at the full-moon-so bright in the pure sky-and then jumped down. Slowly and stately, he walked through the double row of green plants, reached the stairs and... started going down.

[1]. A Calcutta daily paper, in English.

[2]. "So glaube ich heute Im Sinne des allmächtigen Schöpfers zu handeln" (" Mein Kampf," edit. 1935. p. 70)

[3]. "Der völkischen Weltanschauung muss es im völkischen Staat endlich gelingen, jenes edlere Zeltalter herbeizufüren, in dem die Menschen ihre Sorge nicht mehr in der Höherzüchtung von Hunden Pferden und Katzen erblicken sondern im Emporheben des Menschen selbst..."("Mein kampf," edit. 1935, P449).

.

Long-Whiskers

CHAPTER IV

THE GREAT ADVENTURE.

At the third foot-step which he took downwards, it seemed as though Long-whiskers hesitated: he seated himself down in the middle of the stairs as he had sat upon the window-sill: his front-paws stretched out, his head erect or gracefully bent down : looking up, at the moon, and then down, into the dark, silent court-yard. Who knows ? Perhaps he would not have gone down at all-not on **that** night, at least-if something had not happened.

He suddenly saw Heliodora's tall, white form walking along the verandah towards the winding stairs; towards **him**. And she was calling him : " My puss ! my beautiful one !" She wanted him to come back. She was aware that something unusual, perhaps something tragic, something irreparable was about to happen. And she was trying to prevent it. She now saw the splendid cat upon the third step of the stairs, seated like a sphinx in full moonlight. She could not help stopping a second to admire him. He **was** a beauty,-that ordinary gutter-cat that she had picked up as a starving kitten, over a year and a half before ! It was, in a way, a pity to disturb him; to call him back against his will (no one knew better than she did that cats have a will of their own) ; to draw him out of the dream-like phosphorescent light that he seemed to be enjoying. And yet... suppose he did go down and get lost, and have to seek his food in the dust-bins, as his mother once used to, after all these months of comfort and security. **That** would doubtless be worse than being forcibly drawn away from his moon-light contemplation ! So she walked towards him, determined to catch hold of him and carry him back.

First she called him once more in her most loving voice: the voice he had so often answered by rubbing his big round head against her, and purring. This time, he heard the sweet voice, but he neither moved nor purred. Those soft intonations of the two-legged creatures' speech were, -had always been, as far as he possibly could remember, -connected in his feline consciousness, with all the life which his inner urge was now precisely prompting him to forsake. To listen to their call and turn back was to renounce the new life in moon-light and freedom- in the vastness of the unknown earth. " My puss ! My beautiful puss ! My purring velvet ! " the voice repeated. The round glossy head looked up to the familiar two-legged form, for there was a fascination in that voice. And had Heliodora then stood still, who can tell ? Perhaps the cat would have slowly got up and walked back, against his deeper urge, to the home where he was loved. But, in her haste to keep him from running to his ruin, she continued walking towards him and stepped onto the narrow landing. Then she stooped down and stretched out her arms to the moonlit feline. Long-whisker suddenly ran down the winding stairs, as fast as he could, as though panic-stricken. Heliodora ran down a few steps in pursuit of him, but soon came up again. She knew she could not run as fast as a cat- especially as Long-whiskers; it was no use trying.

She remained a long time leaning over the low verandah wall, looking into the dark court-yard where the cat had disappeared. " My poor, beautiful puss," she kept on thinking; "you don't know **where** you are running !" An unsurmountable feeling of powerlessness oppressed her. " Every animal, every plant, has its destiny, like every person and every kin ," she reflected; " its destiny: the mathematical result of millions of former lives, that nothing can change. I have done my best. Now go your way, my poor furry sphinx ! Go your way, since you must -in order to live and learn, as we all do ! '"

And she suddenly remembered the war that was taking a bad turn-now in September, 1943-and she thought of the thousands of men and women of good Nordic blood, enemies of National Socialist Germany, who were also "going their way," the way of perdition, deaf to the Fuhrer's call. And tears welled up to her eyes as the feeling of utter powerlessness grabbed her once more.

On that night, after many and many weeks, Sadhu came and stretched himself at her side and purred and purred as she stroked him. But she thought of poor Long-whiskers wandering along the lanes, further and further away from the peaceful home, towards some nightmarish fate, and she thought of the immeasurably broader world-tragedy that she was equally unable to prevent, and could not fall asleep.

*   *   *

Long-whiskers at any rate, was at first most happy. As he had reached the bottom of the stairs, he had heard a noise and been afraid and gone and hidden himself behind a heap of empty cases in the corner of the yard. But he had soon decided that it had been but a " false alarm," and walked out. The yard was closed. At the lower edge of the door, however, a part of a plank was missing. The cat crept through the hole, ran along the passage that led into the street, turned left, and found himself in another, no less broad artery: that self-same Dharmatala Street along which Heliodora had carried him, a thin, half-starved kitten, over a year and a half before. He wanted to run across it, to the opposite foot-path. A car that came rushing by made him change his mind. Long-whiskers did not remember ever having seen such a thing as a car (or any vehicle, at that) and therefore he was scared. He ran into the dark lane, past the go-down in which he mewed and mewed in which he had once so desperately answer to his mother's repeated calls-and passed the house in the back-yard of which, in a cow-shed, he and his brother and two sisters had come into the world, on a night like this. As he realised that there was no danger, he gradually stopped running. But he continued to follow the lane at a fairly fast tempo. The white parts of his coat gleamed whiter than ever, and the black ones blacker and glossier by contrast, as he walked through patches of moon-light. The air was cool-it was in September[1] and sweet-scented, in spite of the occasional heaps of refuse that one came across as one went. The smell of trees, of grass, brought by the wind from distant Chowringhee Avenue, and from the Maidan; the smell of incense from some house-window or from some shop not yet closed (where a few sticks of it were burning before some crude picture or painted statue of Goddess Lakshmi, or of elephant-headed Ganesh) ; the smell of the earth itself prevailed over every stench. And Long-whiskers experienced a feeling of well-being, of power, of intensified life, as he walked along-free !-into the Unknown: a feeling that he had missed during his long months of sheltered life in Heliodora's room or in her lap. He crossed quite a number of emaciated cats such as own mother had once been, scratching about in the dust-heaps for a fishbone or some clot of putrid rice buried in ashes and rotting banana peelings. But he did not notice them: felines are confirmed individualists. And days were yet to pass, many days-before he was to compete with these wretched ones in the struggle for life.

He was free-inhaling the cool air on a moon-lit night and not yet hungry. loving Heliodora and her quiet, cosy room were completely out of his consciousness.

*   *   *

He walked and walked; crossed another broad street; went into another lane at right angles with it. Then suddenly, from some place, a smell of fish reached him (he was now in what the Two-legged ones call the New Market). It was an appetising smell. And for the first time since his departure from Wellesley Street number 1, where Heliodora's lived, a memory of the old home rose in him: a plate of boiled fish and, next to it, a plate of creamy milk set before him. After chewing the fish, he would lap the cream. (Heliodora generally used to give her cats fish mixed with rice. But some of them, such as Sadhu, Long-whiskers, and one or two others, had become finicky after a few weeks and would eat nothing but fish alone. And the woman was weak enough to grant them their desire). But this was but a fleeting memory. Something else soon attracted Long-whiskers' attention; something. . or should we not rather say some**body,** for it was a young she-cat, half his size, but lovely: lithe; serpentine in her gait; and as black as night itself when there is no moon. Her eyes were of a pale, transparent yellow, like those of a panther.

She was sitting upon her hind legs, apparently calm and composed, in front of a door. But as Long-whiskers came nearer, it seemed to him as though she released a faint mew-a mew that meant : " The night is beautiful; and here I am ' "

It was not the first time he had courted a she-cat: there were plenty of them in Heliodora's room, and he had known one or two intimately-an eighteen-month old "tom" is no longer a baby ! But it **was** the first time he was **alone** with one in the moon-light. (The very drawback of the old life in the peaceful home was that one never could be alone. There were too many cats there, and there was no privacy. Long-whiskers had-like all felines-an inborn love of privacy and **freedom**).

He went up to the reduced black panther who was looking at him invitingly-so it seemed to him. But no sooner was she within his reach, than she sprang up and fled. Long-whiskers ran in pursuit of her. They ran-two graceful shadows, one after the other-right through what the Two-legged ones call the New Market and across the square stretches before it, and along Lindsay Street and across Chowringhee Avenue, straight into the immense " Maidan ". Oh ! what a splendid place, this Calcutta Maidan ! There was grass there-grass, grass, and still further grass. And the place was limitless.

Long-whiskers caught up his lady-love and fastened his mouth to the back of her neck, to keep her down. But she struggled herself away from his hold-a feline lady-love is not so easy to conquer ! She ran a few foot-steps away from him and then... mewed an unmistakable mew of solicitation and rolled herself in the grass before him so as to say : " I am beautiful; I am desirable. Come ! " " Prrrrr " answered Long-whiskers. And he came. The miniature black panther was lying upon her back. Long-whiskers licked the soft fur of her belly. But just at that moment the coquettish she-cat jumped up ran away, only to stop again some twenty yards further and again to roll in the grass, calling for love,-and again to run away as soon as the lover was about to take her. At last, however,-after many an unsuccessful leap and further and further galloping in the moon-shine,-Long-whiskers overcame her faked resistance and possessed her... far away from the city and its night rumours; far away from other cats no less than from the Two-legged species; right in the middle of the grassy " Maidan " under the bright round Moon and the hardly visible stars. He forgot himself, and she-his black silky panther-forgot herself. Their individualities ceased for a while to exist, and in him, the eternal He-Cat, Creator and Lord of everything, and in her, the co-eternal, sphinx-like, dark Feline Mother, Lady of all Life, once more mingled their opposite polarities and took consciousness of their double Godhead, as they had been doing for millions and millions of years. And once more the divine spark-the creative Lightning flashed through their furry bodies, and the daily miracle took place: there was life in the female's womb. Sixty-five days later, two, three or four more baby-cats would be born to struggle and misery-to the horrid life of the Calcutta street animal. They would know practically nothing save hunger and fear; no love, save that of their unfortunate mother, for a few brief weeks. And yet...they would fulfil the purpose which the divine Cat has assigned to them from all eternity: they would in spite of all carry Catdom a generation further-its ever-lastingness.

*   *   *

Long-whiskers woke up in the ditch in which he had spent the rest of the night,-fast asleep after his exhaustion. He stretched himself and got up. He must have slept a long time, for the sun was hot. He felt hungry. But there was, within his reach, nothing he could eat: not a mouse, not a mole, not even a lizard or a cockroach. Of course, he could have tried to go back to the home of plenty where he had spent all but the first six weeks of his life. There was a lot of nice fresh fish to be had there; and a comfortable lap to lie in, when one wanted to rest and was in a mood to be stroked. He still would have found his way back. But the home of plenty had walls. And he had just had the taste of wild life-of **real** life-in limitless space. His tame-cat's inner voice told him: " Go back ! " but his wild-cat's inner voice said : "No ! walk on ! The world is wide. And there is adventure ! " His tame-cat's consciousness had awakened hardly four thousand years before. But his wild-cat's consciousness was a hundred or perhaps a thousand times as old as that, and had, therefore, a stronger grip upon him. He let it take the lead of his life. And he slowly started walking, apparently without an aim, as the free cats, his ancestors, had walked through the high grasses and ferns, in the days in which there were yet no two-legged mammals on earth.

He went along the road that leads to Kidderpur,-for how long ? Who can tell ? He walked and walked, but found nothing to eat. The sun was hotter and hotter. And Long-whiskers felt the pangs of hunger, more and more. He was also beginning to feel tired: he could hardly lift his paws. He lay down in the grass on the side of the road, to rest for a while. Had Heliodora passed by at that very moment and stooped to pick him up, he would have, without resistance, let her carry him back to the old home and no doubt purred in her arms all the way. Perhaps he was making up his mind to try to walk back there, even now, in spite of all. He was so hungry ! For the time being, however, he lay in the grass. He had never yet walked such a long way in all his life, and his paws and joints were aching. He would start his return-journey in a few minutes, when he felt better.

But just then three or four children-boys ten or twelve years old-came walking past. They probably would not have noticed him in the grass had he not, in his innocence of this wicked world, gone out of his way to call their attention. But he was hungry, as I have said already. And all these months he had known no other Two-legged ones besides kind and loving Heliodora. The fears and hardships of his far-gone kittenhood he had completely forgotten. And so, not knowing better, he held long-legged ones in general for helpful creatures. And as he saw the children coming nearer and nearer, he mewed-a feeble, discrete mew that meant: "Do give me something to eat, "-On hearing which one of the boys (a nasty brood, the lot of them) shouted: " Oh ! a cat ! " and, picking up a sharp stone, flung it at Long-whiskers. A shriek of pain followed the beseeching and friendly mew. The stone had hit the cat on the back of his neck and opened a deep wound in the glossy coat. The children laughed as Long-whiskers now a wiser cat in his estimation of the two-legged species -fled from them as fast as he could. For a long time, wherever the cat went, drops of blood marked his passage.

In the happy little room where she had been feeding the other cats, Heliodoza was thinking of Lang-whiskers; praying that no harm should happen to him. Since his departure, she had been thinking of him all the time. And as she recalled the callousness and cruelty of most human beings-of those of the inferior races at least-towards animals, she uttered for the millionth time the prayer she had been addressing the heavenly powers from her earliest childhood onwards : "Treat men, individually and collectively, as they treat animals: strike those who hit them; torture those who torture them; kill those who kill them. Also work Thy divine vengeance upon all those who consider crimes against innocent life-against beasts and trees with approval or even with indifference. And help me to be an instrument of Thy justice !

Long-whiskers wandered for days and days, with his bleeding neck. The wound was hurting him more and more. He could not lick it, and flies would constantly sit in it and worry him to death. In addition to that, he was always hungry.

He now avoided the Two-legged ones as much as he could. He would run and hide himself under a waiting cart or motor-car; in a gutter between two houses; up an occasional tree or stair-case; or upon a roof, if there happened to be one within his reach, and across other roofs, till he found a crack to slip into-as soon as he saw one of them who seemed to him as though he were walking towards him. And he soon learnt that the young devils are even worse than the elder ones. However, this distinction was not rigorously reliable. It was prudent to keep out of the way of the whole horrible brood, and to wander in quest of one's food at dead of night, when its specimens are mostly asleep. So, four days after his first tragic adventure, Long-whiskers had managed to jump into some ground-floor kitchen between two and three a.m., and there, to push off the lid of a saucepan and to lap as much milk as is famishing belly could hold. He had then slept -in the space between the inner wooden beams and the outer corrugated-iron roofing of the kitchen,-a sound, dreamless sleep, not broken by pangs of hunger: his first happy sleep since the night he had left Heliodora's room. But when he had, on the following night, crawled out of his hiding place (which could only be reached from outside) jumped upon the dust-bin in the court-yard, and from there tried to get into that kitchen once more through the window-bars, he had found the shutters closed. And as there was no other way of getting in, he had roamed about the next day and night; he had come back to the kitchen-window and again found it shut; he had roamed and roamed until, at last, he had found some scraps of fried fish in a dust-heap. The fish was good, but it had been thrown upon decaying vegetables, sour rice and other kitchen refuse. It was half-covered with ashes. Yet Long-whiskers-who in his months of plenty would never have touched such food,-gulped it down greedily... and felt better.

He gradually got into the habit of searching for his food in dust-bins and refuse-heaps. Once, a kind old man who was sitting in front of a sweet-shop, called him-"Billi, billi, billi'[2] . puss, puss, puss... "-and offered him a little milk in an earthen cup, on the floor. Poor Long-whiskers smelt the good warm milk, but was afraid to come near. The old man looked harmless enough. But there were other people about the place, and among them young boys going in and out the shop and walking along the foot-path. The cat,-that now had a scar at the back of his neck remembered the sharp stone, the pain, and those other boys' devilish laughter... and he ran as fast as his legs could carry him. And this was not the first time that fear had proved itself in him even stronger than hunger-fear, that everyday experience of stray animals, in cities and villages where human being a have lost their sense of duty towards other creatures, or never had it: that curse of innocent life in a man-ridden world in which man is a devil most of times.

Within a few weeks he had become skin and bone,- like most of the Calcutta street-cats. His coat, once so thick and shiny, had become matted and dull. The hair would not grow again over his scar. Had Heliodora been able to see him, it is difficult to say whether she would have recognised him or not. His only happy moments were those during which he was courting some she-cat, as thin and miserable as himself, and possessing her upon some roof or in some lonely back-yard in the moon-light, or those which he spent in the unconsciousness of sleep.

But worse times were still in store for him. One night, he caught a rat: a big, fat gutter-rat that would have provided the best meal he had managed to secure himself for a very long time. But it was not as easy as it looked to kill such a huge creature outright. The rat, even after it could no longer

run, struggled bravely till the end and, before dying, stuck his sharp teeth into the cat's lips and tore the flesh asunder. Bleeding, Long-whiskers had to let go. The rat expired at his feet. But the cat could not eat him. He could not open his mouth, for pain. His lower lip that the rat had torn in two, was swelling. He remained all night in the gutter, shivering with fever, by the side of the dead rat, and, as morning dawned, tried to drag his prey into a hiding place: a narrow space between two " walls " of corrugated iron; a sewer between two rows of "houses" practically touching each other, in a " bustee "[3] not far from the three-storeyed stone house where Heliodora lived-his many wanderings had brought him back there, three months after his departure. But before he could succeed in doing so, a daring kite came and snatched the dead rat away from him. Poor Long-whiskers snarled and spat, but could do no more. He retreated into the malodorous "corridor"-which was cool and quiet at least (the entrance was too narrow for Two-legged ones to come in) and remained there the whole day, crouching against the rusty "wall," hungry and in pain.

Hours passed. The cat did not move. Pain was stronger than hunger. Fleeting impressions-greater or lesser noise behind the metallic " walls "; greater or lesser heat; more or less light from the sky above-gave the cat a vague account of the course of the Sun in heaven and of life in the immediate surroundings. But pain remained the overwhelming sensation: the one that Long-whiskers could neither dismiss nor suppress. He grinned and bore it in silence, as only animals do, besides those men who are more than men. And the colour of the sky above changed. The metallic "walls" became less hot. Another evening was coming. Long-whiskers was still crouching in the same place.

Then something unusual occurred: he saw several cats walk past him-first, a fat, aggressive, stripy " tom ", then a she-cat who walked heavily, for she was expecting half-a-dozen kittens; then another she-cat- a lovely young black velvety creature, like the one he had possessed on that night in the moon-lit " Maidan," his first night out-then, two more " toms," one white and yellow, the other all white but for a touch of grey on his head and on the tip of his tail. Never had he witnessed such a procession of felines-and all well-fed ones, not poor wretches like himself, with every bone jutting out under a dull, scanty fur. They all seemed to be going to the same place, as though they had an appointment. What place could that be ? One in which there was food every day ? Or one in which pain no longer existed ? Poor Long-whiskers was so hungry-and his poor, swollen lip was hurting him so much ! As though some new, happy destiny were guiding him from within, he made an effort and got up, and followed the privileged cats.

The narrow passage along which they walked led to a low stone wall surmounted by a railing. One had to jump up and go through, and jump down again. The way beyond smelt of wood. It was, in fact, bordered on both sides with heaps and heaps of fresh-cut planks. And one could hear noises-sawing and banging-as one went along it, although one seldom met a two-legged creature and never saw any of them at work.

Long-whiskers had followed the cats more than half the way when he noticed that they all suddenly took to running. Somewhere, far away, one could now distinguish the sound of a voice : " Puss, puss, puss; my pussy, pussy, pusses ! My silky ones, my furry ones ! Puss, puss, puss! "

Long-whiskers could not understand the human speech. Yet the **tone** of those words when not the words themselves worked upon him like a spell, stirring deep, forgotten memories long buried in unconsciousness. He looked inquiringly at a huge ginger "tom" whom he had managed to catch up with, as though to ask him: " Where are you all going at such a speed ? " In the meantime the voice was heard again : " My pussy, pussy, pusses " The huge ginger-coloured "tom" leaped forward with a peculiar mew of joyous affection. And Long-whiskers, who was well-versed in feline language-seized the meaning of **that** mew : **" We are going to the Two-legged Goddess**. Hark ! She is calling us ! "

His heart filled with a vague anticipation, he leaped in his turn over the dilapidated stone wall and into the path that so strongly smelt of timber, and finally reached the courtyard, into which it gave access. There, in a glow of sunset, actually stood a tall white female figure: a Two-legged one, admittedly, but not one like most of them. Some twenty cats had already gathered around her, mewing and rubbing their glossy heads against her legs. The big ginger "tom" had even seated himself upon her shoulders ! She put down two huge dishes out of which came an appetising smell of fish. The ginger tom at once jumped down, and took his place at one of these, along with over a dozen other cats. Then, out of a jug, the woman poured milk into a number of earthen bowls, and watched the cats drink. Now and then she would stroke one of the felines, or pick one up (one that had finished eating and drinking) and press him in her arms. Her face was stamped with an infinite sadness which was far beyond the animals' understanding, and which they therefore did not notice. But they **did** feel the love that poured from her dark eyes ; her particular radiance, which stilled all fear; and the magic of her touch, which made a cat wish to seat himself in her lap and purr himself to sleep.

Long-whiskers who had, at first, remained crouching in a corner, aloof from the other cats, got up and walked towards one of the dishes of fish and rice (Not that he **could** eat. with his torn lip ! But perhaps he would try, all the same. He **was** so hungry, and the fish smelt so nice !) But the cats growled at him,- the newcomer. And the huge ginger " tom," so healthy and strong that he gave the impression of a miniature tiger, even slapped him upon the head with one of his heavy paws. The woman then took a little food out of the dish and placed it apart, upon a slab of stone, for him. Long-whiskers saw her two hands stretch out to catch hold of him. Automatically, he made a move to flee. But no; he could not. Something invisible, stronger than the old fear of the two-legged species, kept him on the spot. He merely put back his ears and crouched, as the hands picked him up and gently put him down near the appetising food. He smelt it. He even started purring. But not eat. His swollen lip ached. He turned towards the woman his great transparent green eyes-all that was left of his former beauty -and gave out a faint mew. The woman looked at him intently, and took him in her arms. In the wretched skeleton which he had become, she had not at once recognised her splendid Long-whiskers. But she now considered his face: the regular black markings round the eyes, separated by a white, spear-like patch, were the same. It could not **but** be he. But in what a state ! Tears welled up to the dark human eyes that looked into his, and the human lips put a kiss upon his poor, whirling head. The cat felt an overwhelming tenderness pour into him from that strange two-legged being.

Something was taking place within his dim consciousness. It was not the awakening' of a clear memory such as those which human creatures have; not the **thought** of " her "- kind, loving Heliodora; for it **was** she indeed, whom he had found again after those three months in the hell of hunger and fear, but the **feeling** of her; the coming to life of the old sensation of pleasure at her touch and of safety in her lap: a certitude of his flesh that hunger and fear were over, over for ever, because she-the " Presence " of all-powerful Love was there again. Well did those street-cats that gathered every day in that and other court-yards to eat the fish and rice which she cooked for them, call her, in their inexpressible language: " the Two legged goddess " !

*　　*　　*

Long-whiskers relaxed in the loving arms. He now felt he was moving:-being carried away. While he stretched himself across Heliodora's breast, he had the impression of fleeting lights and shadows, and patches of colour passing by before his half-closed eyes. It was just as when long ago; before those hellish weeks had seemed to have put an end to the old life,-she had been carrying him in the same position up and down her room, until he had purred himself to sleep... He felt, with undefinable delight that the old life was mysteriously beginning again- or perhaps just continuing, after an awful nightmare. And he purred louder, as the woman pressed him more tenderly to her bosom, whispering, now and then, in a subdued voice that melted his heart, (he could not make out why) : "My poor, dear cat ! My beautiful furry pet ! What **have** you become ? "

She was now walking upstairs, still with him in her arms. The lighting, the smell of the old wooden stair-case were the same as long ago. Yes, it had all been a dream, felt Long-whiskers as Heliodora stepped at last into the old, familiar room full of cats, and closed the door behind her.

Every trace of his great adventure now faded out of his

consciousness, completely. There was nothing more to remind him of it, save his aching lip-and that was rapidly healing. Not being a Two-legged one, Long-whiskers did not connect the occasional pain with his whole recent past, but merely with the rat that had bitten him. And even that rat was becoming more and more shadowy, more and more remote, and was soon to vanish into oblivion... while old sensations and old habits set in again.

1. At the end of the rainy season.

2. "Billi," in Rindusthani, means `'" cat."

3. An Indian slum.

CHAPTER V

PEACEFUL DEATH AND REBIRTH.

There were many more cats than before in Heliodora's room: some of the old ones (among which, Long-whiskers' mother) had had kittens; and there were a number of new ones-outsiders. Many were sick. Many had died, owing to a recent epidemic of " feline distemper ", soon to be replaced by the newcomers rescued from the streets.

Long-whiskers was soon a happy cat once more. His lip had entirely healed, thanks to some ointment that Heliodora had applied upon it, and he now ate without difficulty. And he was more than ever attached to the woman. She only needed to look at him for him to start purring, and to jump into her lap, if he was not already lying there. Then she would stroke his emaciated back, and he would purr louder. Something within him told him that wherever " she " was, there was safety, good food and gentle care; that all fear could not but disappear at her touch. He worshipped her,- without knowing and without caring who she was in that mysterious world of the Two-legged mammals, with its problems, its wars and its ideologies, all as far beyond his understanding as angels' and gods' affairs are beyond human speculation, if angels and gods there be.

And yet he was not destined to live long at her side. In spite of good food, his coat was not getting back its former shine. His body remained thin. Then his appetite decreased and his nose started running. And Heliodora recognised in him the well-known first symptoms of " feline distemper " -the incurable disease that had carried away already so many of her cats. Whether Long-whiskers had caught the germs of that disease during his wanderings or just now, from other sick cats to which she had given shelter, she did not know. But she knew what was the matter with him, and knew also that there was nothing to be done: the "vet" had told her so, on so many other occasions. The medicine he gave could at most postpone the animal's end. And Long-whiskers did not like taking medicine. However -in order to feel that she had done "all she could"- Heliodora forced the prescribed dose down his throat at the prescribed intervals, until the little bottle was finished. Every time, the cat would struggle himself out of her grip and run into some corner (generally under the book-case) until the taste of the potion had vanished from his mouth. But as, after a week or so, she gave him the last spoonful, he did not run away. Instead, he looked at her with entreating eyes, so as to say: "Why do you torment me with this stuff that I don't like ? Can't you let me die in peace ?" And Heliodora understood.

She gave him no more medicine. It could not have saved him, anyhow. But she gave him all her love, to the end. And this made his cat's life worth living, even in its decline. And it bound him to her-as a spark of the One divine Life to another more brilliant spark of the same; a spark more aware of its divinity; more awake, but by no means more divine than he-for ever.

Long-whiskers ate less and less, and soon lost the little weight he had, at first, put on. His nose and throat, continually stuffed, tormented him. And so did the loathsome digestive troubles that are another of the features of " feline distemper ". Yet he was happier, much happier than in the days of constant fear. He had become too weak to jump into Heliodora's lap, but he only had to look up and faintly mew: she knew what it meant, and would at once take him up as gently as she could, and let him lie in her arms or upon her knees, and stroke him. A feeble purr, which often brought tears into the woman's eyes, was the cat's answer.

At last, one day, as the poor beast was lying as usual upon a cushion in a basket-and the other cats here and there, all about the room, Heliodora thought she had heard a disquieting sound: something like a smothered groan. She got up and went to the basket. She lay her hands upon the once so sleek, now so emaciated creature, in whose body she had noticed a slight stir. Was it the beginning of the end ?-already ? The soft, silky paws were already cold; and Long-whiskers was breathing heavily. With infinite care, fearing that the slightest jerk might hurt him, Heliodora picked him up, cushion and all, lay him upon her lap, and let one hands rest upon his head while she stroked him with the other. The head made an effort to turn itself towards her ; the large, yellowish-green eyes gazed at her with a yearning that she had never seen in them before, and she felt the familiar purr-the answer to her love- under the neck that was already stretching itself in the struggle of coming death. Then the legs started moving, as the head kept turning from one side to the other. Tears welled up to the woman's eyes : " My poor, dear cat," she whispered " you are at least dying in my arms: happy-loved in the end, and beyond the end '"

She thought of the millions of stray- animals that die in the streets of towns and villages without ever having experienced the touch of human love; she thought of the hunted or trapped creatures, and of those that die in torture for the sake of man's criminal lust of sacrilegious research, and of those that are slaughtered every day to become butcher's meat. And that atrocious feeling of powerlessness beyond all hope that had oppressed her so many times in the course of her life, overwhelmed her once more. The one State in which vivisection was treated as a crime was now struggling for its life against the whole world. What could **she**, Heliodora, do besides helping that State in its war-effort, directly or indirectly, by any means she could think of, and... helping a few cats and dogs to live outside the hell of fear, and to end their lives in peace ?

Her warm hands gently treated upon the furry body, gradually getting colder and colder in the throes of death. "My poor cat," thought the Friend of animals, "**if** it be within my power to influence that Unknown which comes afterwards if anything comes,-may you have, this time -a better incarnation "

As for Long-whiskers, it is, without the **experience** of death, difficult to say what he felt, as life slowly ebbed out of him. It seemed to Heliodora as though his eyes, already dim, tried a last time to gaze at her through the cloud that was setting down upon them. His last yearning, his last expression of consciousness before all sense of " separate " existence- still outside the great Ocean of Sleep-left him, was " Oh ! to see " her " To see " her "-and feel " her" touch once more ! "

And thus he died, in the old peaceful home that had welcomed him as a helpless kitten; in the loving arms of the woman who had brought him there for the second time, out of the hell of hunger and fear. Heliodora buried him at night, at the foot of a tree, in Wellington Square.

*   *   *

He took birth again as a most lovely, stripy, ginger-coloured kitten, in London, near Waterloo Station, among kind and good English people: father, mother and four year-old little girl. He had a ginger-and-white brother, and a tortoise-shell coloured sister His mother lay in a large basket- upon an old pillow, purring as the human mother stroked her and as her three silky babies sucked her, their front paws moving regularly, as their tiny round heads hung at her paps.

" We can't keep all three;- unfortunately we can't in such times as these " the woman was saying. " But we shall keep one and try to find good homes for the other two. Aunty Rose told me she wants one, anyhow…"

" I want that one one ! " cried little Elsie, pointing out to the young stripy tom. I want him for my Christmas present. And I'll call him Sandy."

And so, Sandy remained while his brother and sister were given, in course of time, to Aunty Rose and to another cat-loving friend of the Harrington family. Loved, well-fed in spite of the food restrictions (he was born in December 1943), pampered by everyone in the house, specially by little Elsie, who insisted upon his sleeping in (or at least upon) her bed, he grew into an enormous cat, as beautiful as Long-whiskers had ever been, and nearly twice as big. As the Harringtons had no garden, but lived on the ground floor, he was allowed to take a stroll once a day, in the late evening, when passers-by were few. The rest of the time he spent upon a cushion in the drawing-room, or in Mrs. Harrington's lap, or in little Elsie's arms-or in the kitchen when it was food time. He was as happy as a " doctored " cat can be.

PART II

GINGER

CHAPTER VI.

HELIODORA'S HOMEWARD JOURNEY.

The Sun was slowly going down. The steamer had not yet started. Heliodora stood upon the deck, leaning against the railing and looking over the port of Bombay that she was soon to leave.

Never had there been such an overcrowded ship. It was carrying over six thousand British soldiers with their officers, apart from its civilian passengers,-all first class ones by compulsion, as all other classes were requisitioned for the home-bound troops.

People were coming and going on the deck: members of the crew, walking past in a hurry; passengers and passengers' friends, standing, sitting, talking ; members of the British forces in uniform,-swarms of them!-porters, carrying luggage upon their heads or upon their backs. But Heliodora was more alone than she would have been in the midst of a desert. She stood, immobile, her elbows upon the railing, her head in her hands, lost in her thoughts. And these thoughts of hers had nothing in common with those of any of the men or women that were standing or sitting all round her, or that passed by, like shadows.

Her mind wandered back to the time she had first landed in India, some fourteen years before, full of the lure of the land that " worships Aryan Gods to this very day "; full of juvenile enthusiasm, inspite of the fact that she was then already twenty-six; full of tremendous hopes and illusions. She remembered herself watching the Vaishakha Purnima procession in the endless torch-lit corridors of the Rameshwaram temple, or gazing, from the Rock of Trichinopoli, at the Kauveri valley, with the twenty-eight " gopurams " of the Sriringam Temple merging out of the tropical vegetation; she remembered herself wandering all over India, from the extreme south to the Himalayas and from Punjab and Kashmir to the eastern border of Assam, addressing crowds in the open,- before vast expanses of rice fields and coconut palms or desert-like, almost Central

Asian landscapes,- and telling them, over and over again: " The message of Aryan pride and of dutiful, passionless warlike action, which the seers and bards of old have handed down to you,-the message of Lord Krishna in the sublime Song[1]-that is our message," and quoting " Mein Kampf " and the "   Myth of the Twentieth Century " along with the eternal words of the Sanskrit Writ. And she remembered how, every time the dusky crowds had cheered her,- those dusky crowds in the midst of which a few fairer faces with perfect Aryan features always bore witness to the blood of the immemorial Northern invaders, builders of Sanskrit-speaking India-the grand German song " and **tomorrow the whole World** ."[2] had come back to her mind, and how she had felt proud to contribute, in her own strange way, to the fulfilment of the dream it implied.

Now the glorious dream had proved to be but a dream, - or at least, she then thought so. She was about to sail towards a continent in ruins and, which is more, towards a continent in which the Dark Forces were to remain in power for God alone knew how long.

She recalled the peaceful home where she had spent so many years-her cats, lying in the huge flower-pots in the shade on the verandah, or upon the cool Floor of her room, under the fan, or in her lap, or upon her bed. Where were they all, now, those loving felines that she had picked up from the streets of Calcutta, and fed and pampered ? Most of them were dead, (there had been two consecutive epidemics of " feline distemper " before she had left) ; two - velvety Sadhu, and Lalu, a big stripy yellow cat,-were still in the two rooms, in the care of Heliodora's most trusted friend and collaborator; the remainder, some twenty of them, had had to be given away. Heliodora had been assured that they would be taken good care of. But who could ever love them as she had ? Would she ever see any of them again, if she one day came back ? Something deep within her bosom told her definitely: " No."

Then **why** was she going away, leaving everything that had been part and parcel of her life for so many years ? What was she planning to do, among the ruins of Europe ? What was she expecting to find there, which was worth while her leaving everything in order to seek it ? Heliodora could not

60

have answered that question. Her conscious self did not know **what** was urging her to go. She only knew the urge did not come from her, but sprang from Something by far greater than she, Something of which she was but a **part**, and which compelled her, as the brain compels the finger, the elbow or the foot, parts of the body. It came from the great collective Self into which she had merged her tiny individuality years and years before; from that great collective Self with which she stood or fell, whatever she did. She could not even have chosen to disobey- for the great collective Self **was** her own self. She was sailing in order to **live** the horror of defeat along with the others, with all the unknown comrades who still shared her Hitler faith, she who had never seen them at the height of glory, nor even seen the hallowed Leader who was also **hers.** And nothing- not even the peaceful home; not even loving Sadhu and the other cats that used to lie and purr in her lap,- nothing, I say, could hold her back.

The siren started and Heliodora shuddered. So, she really **was going !** Going where ? The headlines of a newspaper that had caught her glance in a railway carriage, some six months before, "Berlin is an inferno," suddenly came back to her mind, with all the bitterness of the lost war. And she felt tears welling up to her eyes: tears of utter despair. But she had to go.

The Sun was now setting, and the waters of the bay lay in a splendour of golden night. The siren resounded once more over their length and breadth. And the ship started moving. Heliodora remained on the upper deck, her eyes fixed upon the receding coast-line. The wind shuffled her auburn locks, which took on shades of fiery reddish-yellow in the evening glow.

*   *   *

As she came downstairs, she was given a form to fill. In late 1945, filling forms was as tiresome and necessary an occupation as eating and drinking. Heliodora glanced through the usual words in their usual order: name, surname, date and place of birth, profession... religion, etc.

She did not know, did not ask, did not care to know **why** one wanted all this information about her. But at the item "religion", she started. **That** was an opportunity of defiance,- and the first one officially given her within months and months. That was a challenge to her own fighting spirit, in spite of collective defeat ! Opposite the word "religion" she boldly wrote in black and white, the words " National Socialist," and after having filled the form completely, handed it over with a smile of bitter satisfaction.

An hour later, she was summoned to an office, and stood there before an uniformed Englishman. And the dialogue began:

"**You** filled that form ?" the man asked, after having addressed the woman by her name and surname.

" I did."

"And what is this joke ?" he added, pointing to the unutterable profession of faith.

" It is no joke at all," answered she, with the brazenness of those who have nothing to lose; " this is in fact my religion."

" It is no religion at all, but the most sinister association of criminals that ever existed under the Sun !" " In that case, look upon me also as a 'sinister criminal' for I am proud of being the least of Adolf Hitler's disciples, whatever be the outcome of this damned war," supplied Heliodora with the firmness of unshakable conviction.

" I could get you into serious trouble, but I shall not " answered the purser, or whoever the uniformed man was; " You are not even a German, and you were not in Europe all these years: you don't know what you are saying." The man did not hear, or pretended not to hear, the dedicated woman burst out: "Oh ! yes I do ! And I wish I had the power to prove it." He tore her form in two and then in four, threw the bits into the waste-paper basket, and, handing her a new one, said:

" Now, write it over again, please. And leave out that word... Put down whatever you like, but not **that.** "

" Well," replied she defiantly, " I'll write 'Sun-worshipper,' this time, that is to say: worshipper of Life. **In my eyes, it means the same.** It is not for nothing that our Sign is the eternal Swastika, the Wheel of the Sun. "

After leaving the office, she went back to the deck. And again the thought of the lost war haunted her.

*   *   *

The ship was crowded with people glad to have won the war and glad to be going home: comfortable Englishmen with their families, and British troopers from India and from the Burma and Malaya front. There were some Indians, too. But these were as ready as anyone to speak against dictators in general and Adolf Hitler in particular: a defeated Germany, which they could no longer consider as a handy ally in their struggle against " British imperialism," seemed no longer to interest them. Heliodora recalled the enthusiasm that had, in glorious 1940, greeted in India the news of the march on Dunkirk; and she felt nauseated at the idea of the average human being who always side with the victors, always swallows their propaganda as though it were the truth, for no other reason that they happen to be the victorious. Would she find such people in Europe also- even in Germany, if she managed to get there ? Even among those who had once acclaimed her Führer at the great Party rallies ? Was it for them that she had left everything, including her cats ?

She felt depressed. She hardly spoke to anybody. In the daytime, seated in a corner of the hall, she busied herself with a book she had begun to write in defence of animals. Nothing shocked her so much as the contrast between that interminable fuss made over so-called " war crimes " and " war criminals " and the indifference of the bulk of " decent people " to the daily horrors perpetrated upon dumb four-legged creatures, in the name of food, luxury, sport, scientific research, etc If thousands of beautiful, healthy animals could be made to suffer and to die for the sake of " saving human beings " (and diseased ones at that), then surely a few thousands or even millions of dangerous saboteurs, or sympathisers of such ones, could be wiped out for the defence of better mankind, fighting, during this war, for its very survival, against the coalesced fury of the whole world. She hated that world that dared beg for her sympathy in favour of the " poor" Jews, and that had not yet been able to do away with vivisection and with slaughter-houses. And as she thought of the only State that had suppressed the first of these abominations and whose inspired Ruler had also dreamed of abolishing the second- had been, at least, the only vegetarian ruler in the West- she felt bitter. That State now lay in ruins, and the god-like Leader was dead.

Then somebody would switch on the radio, and out would come either some jazz music, or some silly American love-song- the standard expression of that ugly, boring world, into which Heliodora was being plunged, after all those years of vain struggle and vain hopes,-or... even worse: some Allied-sponsored emission in which such sentences as " systematic de-nazification and re-education of the German people," the " awakening in them of a sense of shame at the thought of the unheard-of crimes which they tolerated, " and "the gradual re-integration of Germany into the community of Christian and democratic nations..." came back over and over again, as **leitmotivs**. And each and every fibre in Heliodora's being was tense with revolt at the sound of those words.

Until late in the night, while the other passengers remained in the sitting-room playing cards, listening to music, or talking, the woman whom the Calcutta cats had called, in their mysterious language, " the Two-legged goddess," would keep leaning against the railing, on the upper-deck, alone, the wind in her face, her eyes fixed upon the starry sky and the deep dark sea without end:

" Les deux goufres ne font qu'un abîme sans bornes de tristesse, de paix, et a d'éblonuisement..."[3]

The verses of the French poet[4] rang in her memory as she breathed the solemnity of infinite space. And she longed for a world without man- a world in which desert and jungle, and the elder mammals, birds and reptiles that dwelt therein, would have reconquered the expanses once usurped by so-called " civilisation "; a world in which big stripy felines would come and drink out of rivers and lakes reflecting palms and enormous ferns, under the moon-light, and in which the whole of human history would be a thing gone for ever, a thing without a trace.

Tels le ciel éclatant et les caux vénérables dorment dans la lumière et dans la majesté, comme si la rumeur des vivants misérables n'avait jamais troublé leur rêve illimité...[5]

But it was not " the living," it was only man that Heliodora would gladly have seen disappear from the surface of our planet. " The living " as a whole, she loved. They were not responsible for the Second World war, nor for the Allied " re-education " schemes. But the destruction of the human species,-under the stars, the voice of the sea; the voice of the wind; the voice of the trees in the storm; the voice of the tigress calling for her mate in the high grasses... **and nothing else !** appeared to her as the only tolerable alternative, after the destruction of the Third German Reich " stronghold and hope of Aryan mankind in the West," as she used to call it. She was totally devoid of the spirit of compromise.

But the sea and the stars and the far-away deserts and jungles, and the howling wind pushing clouds of dust over the ruins of human cities-of those of the Allied Nations as well as of those which the bombers of the Allied Nations had reduced to ashes,- were not yet, alas, the only realities. Even if the wireless had remained silent and even if there had been, on board the ship, neither British troopers to be seen, nor any passengers to discuss current events in her presence, still Heliodora would have known what to expect in post-war Europe. Of course, nobody could " re-educate " her, who had come to the Hitler faith of her own free will, with her eyes wide open, in full consciousness of what she had been doing. But she would now have to witness the slow falling back of thousands of others into the dreary faith centred round " man " - dull, average man- and " suffering humanity ": the faith she so utterly despised; to witness that gradual sinking of what could have been, one day, a continent of supermen; and to witness it, powerless '

She lived on the brink of despair. The faint hope of seeing, one day, the men of Yalta and their supporters, and all those who were then, in 1945, so happy over their " victory," in a worse plight than herself, was the only feeling that prevented her from throwing herself into the sea.

*   *   *

But despair was not all : heresy was worse. And day after day Heliodora felt herself drifting away from the straight, simple path of National Socialist orthodoxy, one of the fundamental traits of which consists in never criticising anything the Führer ever did, said or wrote. To her own horror she was, be it only in the secrecy of her solitary thinking, asking such questions as should not enter the mind of a good disciple, specially of a rank and file one as she was " not even a German ", as the uniformed Englishman had told her, when he had torn up her written profession of faith).

As she leaned, hours long, against the railing of the upper deck,-as far away as she possibly could from jazz music and from B.B.C. comments upon the Allied efforts at " uprooting Nazism,"-problems would worry her ; problems to which there seemed to be no solution, as soon as one ceased to accept Adolf Hitler's will without arguing. " Why, for instance, had the Führer attacked Russia, knowing fully well how difficult it was for Germany to fight on two fronts at the time ? In answer to this, she remembered that British secret envoys had successfully been intriguing with Stalin against Germany. She had gathered this information from some article she had read. And it was as simple an explanation as could be : Stalin had a Jewish wife, whose brothers played an important part in Soviet policy; how could he have resisted the suggestions of the servants of World Jewry in war time ? If Germany had not attacked him, he would have attacked Germany, sooner or later... Molotoff's demands, during the Berlin talks of November, 1940, had been exorbitant anyhow. and war with Russia unavoidable... But then, mercilessly, another question arose ! " Why had the Fuhrer not ordered a few thousands of his parachutists to land in England at the opportune moment, immediately after the Dunkirk retreat ? Why had he during that retreat, ordered his advancing troops to allow a distance of ten kilometres between their vanguard and the fleeing British army ? Obviously, the best thing to do would have been to kill off the whole British Expeditionary Corps, wouldn't it ? Heliodora was no strategist, but she knew that as everybody did. Why had the Fuhrer not taken the easiest.-the only-course to victory ? In vain, she would wrack her brains in order to find out, or to invent, a suitable justification for every decision of his which she could not understand. And then, suddenly, she would realise how far she had gone on the path of rebellion. And she would hate herself for no longer being able to accept the Führer's will and word with all the confidence she once used to, **during** and before the war,- before that defeat which now was, or seemed, a fact for ever.

" Have these slaves of the Jews succeeded in making a bad National Socialist of **me**, of all people ? " thought she, in horror. "For what am I doing just now, but arguing in spirit with our beloved Leader !-I, who was not even in Europe at the time he needed all of us the most I " She would also hate the destroyers of the Third German Reich, and specially the British, to whom Adolf Hitler had stretched out his hand so many times and so sincerely, in genuine effort at peace-making; hate them all the more wildly, as the enormity of her Fuhrer's sacrifice haunted her more and more. She remained in that bitter mood as the ship entered Southampton harbour, and as she, Heliodora, mechanically followed the stream of passengers down the gangway and through the Customs, and into the " boat-train " that carried her to London.

She reached the great city on a cold November night.

1. The Bhagawad-Gita.
2. "... und morgen~ die ganze Welt "
3." The two gulfs make but one fathomnless abyss, of sadness, of peace, and of sparkling light "
4. Leconte de Liale. "Poemes Tragiques." (" *Le Requin*").
5. "Thus, the resplendent sky and the sacred waters are lying asleep in brightness and in majesty, as though the noise of wretched living creatures had never disturbed their endless dream."

CHAPTER VII.

THE CAT'S TEACHING.

Heliodora shivered as she stepped out of the railway carriage and walked along the platform, alone amidst the indifferent crowd. It was not merely the cold, which bit through her inadequate clothing, that sent that strange, icy sensation along her spine. The cold was nothing; she had hardly noticed it. It was not merely sadness at the knowledge that nobody was waiting for her: **that** had no importance ; and she was used to it, anyhow. It was a deep seated feeling of utter powerlessness at the same time as of total revolt that caught hold of her once more, stronger than ever. She knew she was now in London. And that city, that she had visited several times long before, and that she had loved, now appeared to her as nothing more nothing less than the centre from which destruction had descended upon all that had meant anything to her: the starting point of the thousands of bombers which had broken the resistance of the State of her dreams (already before the double wave of converging invaders had closed itself over its smoking ruins). And she loathed the monstrous nest of hypocrisy, blind hatred and stupidity.

Had the finest of those proud S.S. men, whom she looked upon as more-than-human beings, suddenly stood before her and asked her to love the English in spite of all-for the sake of the love which Adolf Hitler had shown them to the very end ; for the sake of the yet unborn generations of theirs, that would, one day (never mind **when**), join the rest of Europe in the tardy exaltation of all he had said and done;- had he, nay, ordered her to love them in her dear Führer's name, she doubtless would have **tried** to obey (for she valued nothing as much as discipline) but probably would have failed to do so. The bitterness that filled her heart would have silenced every other feeling. It already threw a shadow even upon her unconditional faith in the Man she worshipped: as she stepped out of Waterloo Station into the street, she could not help seeing, in every one of the rare passers-by, a person who was **glad** that National Socialist Germany was now crushed. And she would keep on thinking of the soldiers of the British Expeditionary Corps of 1940, and wondering, for the thousandth time, against her better sense: "Why didn't **he** have them all killed off on their way to Dunkirk, and land, and end the war victoriously, then and there …"

No, not even the finest of her German comrades would have succeeded in delivering her from that obsessing, heretical question.

*   *   *

But there were no German National Socialists in England. in 1945, save prisoners of war, all of them away from London,- and no English ones, save a handful of " 18Bs," nearly all in internment. It was not a person that suddenly walked out of the night, straight up to the life-long fighter for Aryan racialism, but... an enormous, ginger-coloured cat-Sandy !

Stately, and supremely graceful, his brushy tail erect, up he came, as though something had been drawing him to that apparently unknown woman. He did not himself realise **what** was attracting him: human beings do not remember their former lives, let alone cats ! But one thing he did realise, and that was that the attraction was irresistible. He started purring as he came nearer the one in whose lap he had so often lain, in days bygone; in whose arms he had died his latest death, nearly two years before. Not that he remembered. I repeat: cats don't. He merely felt as though enchanted at the sight of her, and happier and happier as he entered her field of radiance, and drew nearer and nearer to her.

She caught sight of him and halted in the middle of the lonely foot-path ; put down her suit-case and travelling bag and spoke to the magnificent creature: " My puss ! My stripy velvet ! " He was now at her feet, looking up to her, rubbing his round silky head, with amber-coloured eyes, against her legs. She stooped and stroked him; at the contact of her hand his supple back undulated. She picked him up carefully and held him against her breast. " My purring fur ! " she whispered, as she continued caressing him. He stretched out a powerful paw, and began clawing for pleasure into the wool of her scarf.

How heavy he was ! and how thick and glossy was his coat ! Heliodora suddenly recalled the hundreds of poor, emaciated cats she had been seeing for so many years in the streets of Calcutta and of every Indian town,- and even more so in every town of the Near and Middle East that she knew and in the South of Europe; poor emaciated cats that used to run away at the approach of a human being, and that it used to take days, often weeks to tame, so deep was the terror of man within their blood. This one was obviously well-fed and well-loved. He seemed accustomed to human caresses... And a fact dawned upon the woman's mind- a simple, trivial fact which at once appeared to her as all-important and full of meaning: **this cat belonged to English people, and they were kind to him.**

And what the best among her brothers in faith, what even those whom she revered as her superiors could probably not have achieved at that time,- November, 1945, the innocent beast, utterly unaware of human affairs, did without difficulty: through the mere contrast between his fine condition and that of animals in countries in which Aryan blood is absent, or less pure than in Northern Europe, he gave Heliodora back her **sincere** consciousness of the oneness of the Nordic race, in spite of all the horrors of recent fratricidal war. In a flash, she recalled the godlike Man whose decisions she had dared question, in the secrecy of her mind; whose wisdom she had been on the brink of criticising. " My beloved Führer," thought she, as a tear rolled down her cheek into the cat's warm winter fur, " you were a hundred thousand times right in sparing them at Dunkirk ; you were right in holding out your hand to them to the last. Forgive me my folly. Forgive me my rebellion ! Great One, you were right-always right ! "

And she held Sandy tighter in her arms, and stroked him more lovingly. A sort of silent dialogue took place, on that cold London night, between the dedicated woman and the feline, who had nothing but the testimony of his beauty to oppose to the heaviest accusations against the people among whom he had grown up.

" It is true that **they** started the war," Heliodora could not help thinking, even after her first impulse of reconciliation, for hatred, and specially righteous hatred, is difficult to kill.

" Prrr, prrr, prrr," purred the cat; "but they fed me. They fed me well, in spite of the rationing: see how sleek I am, and what a splendid coat I have ! Prrr, prrr, prrr . They deprived themselves to feed me. They are good people, I tell you "

" It is true that **they** hate all we love," thought the woman. "They hate our Leader; they hate his beloved Germany and her gospel of health, pride and power   ''

" Prrr, prrr, prrr," purred back the cat; "but they love **me**; they love us; they are good and kind to **us**. Prrr, prrr, pzrr, you mustn't hate them, **you cannot hate them, if you love us.**"

"It is true that **they** have destroyed Europe " ... That thought would keep on coming back to Adolf Hitler's disciple. "They have poured streams of fire over Germany; betrayed their own race; identified themselves with its worst enemies..."

" Prrr, prrr, prrr," purred back the cat; "that is because they have been (as they are still being) misled, deceived. But one day they shall wake up from their delusion, turn against their bad shepherds, and help the people of their own blood to build up a new Europe- the very Europe of your dreams, in which we creatures will all be happy- for they are good people at heart; good people like Aryans generally are, taken as a whole. Prrr, prrr, prrr... The roof of it is that they have taken such good care of me ! Prrrrrrrrrr…"

"O Cat, you are right," agreed at last the tough old racialist. "Deeper and more everlasting than what people " do " is what people are: the quality of their blood, which manifests itself in little actions of everyday life. You are right: propagandas come and go; the virtues of the blood remain. "They" were deceived into waging war upon their brothers, but you, my beauty, you they loved spontaneously, without being induced to- because men of their race are naturally inclined to kindness."

And the woman stooped down, lay the cat in her lap, and softly took his big round head in both her hands. And the cat purred and purred, and drew his claws in and out in and out, and nestled against her, as though he had never known any other caresses but hers. Time flew, and passers-by became scarcer and scarcer.

Then, on the ground-floor of a neighbouring house, a door was opened. And in the light that flooded the footpath, Heliodora saw a kind-looking young woman and a six or seven-year old golden-haired little girl. The mother called: " Sandy, Sandy, where are you my pet ?" And the child, pointing to the cat in the stranger's lap, across the street, cried out: " There he is, mummy ! The lady has taken him..." and ran to fetch him. Heliodora, leaving her things where they were, stood up with Sandy in her arms, and carried him back to his owners.

" He is so beautiful that I could not help picking him up and stroking him, " she said. " I love cats "

"And so do we," answered the kind-looking woman. "This one was born at our fire-side some two years ago. He is a beauty, isn't he ?"

" He is my cat," said the child. " He sleeps with me. And his mother sleeps on a cushion in her basket."

The door was closed again. And Heliodora went her way with her suit-case and travelling bag. The night was cold; the future uncertain. She did not even know where she would sleep, just then, let alone how and where she would manage to settle down-and how she would then find an opportunity of going to Germany. But that meeting with the cat that she knew so well, and yet that she could not recognise, had filled her with renewed self-confidence. She was grateful-so grateful-to the lovely and loving beast for having been the instrument of her regaining her old, rigid, National Socialist orthodoxy: that unquestioning acceptance of anything the Führer had said, done or ordered. Thanks to that cat, she now felt sure her Leader was infallible; infallible in spite of defeat; in spite of hundreds of miles of ruins and millions of " displaced persons," not to speak of the dead. Generations of blond, blue-eyed children, as good and kind as the little girl she had just met, would honour him as their invisible Leader, in times yet to come, times without end.

" O Cat," thought she; " had I to learn that from you ?" And she felt small-but strong in spite of all, in the consciousness of unshaken faith.

CHAPTER VIII.

DREARY YEARS.

Sandy could not sleep, that night.

He was a thousand miles away from suspecting that he had just met the mistress he had loved in a former birth Still less did he realise all that their meeting had meant **to her.** (How could he, poor beast ? He had no idea of the war which had caused the death of millions of Two-legged ones and of so many creatures like himself, also. All the inconvenience it had given **him** had consisted in a certain number of trips to the cellar and back, in a basket-in which he had remained fairly quiet in spite of the noise. And as for Heliodora's struggle with herself for the sake of ideological orthodoxy, that was something as far above his comprehension as angels' psychology is beyond that of human beings,- if, of course, there be any such creatures as angels). But he knew that the adventure he had just lived had been **the** great event of his life. This woman was definitely **not** like any of the Two-legged ones whom he had known up till then. There was something powerful in her radiance, something irresistible in her touch; her caresses were not like those of the others: they were more-than physical; they brought into one's fur, and through the fur into one's nerves, magnetic energies from an unknown world; they plunged one into a paradise of fervour and of tenderness beyond all expression- into an ocean of delight in which one lost all sense of time and place, and could only purr and purr, and stretch out one's paws and push out and pull in one's claws rhythmically... as in the far-gone days one had been a fluffy kitten nestling against one's mother's warm coat and drinking her milk; in which one could only purr and claw, purr and claw, and forget everything save the certitude of being alive, and of life being the same as pleasure. And when one half-awoke from one's rapture, and saw those large dark eyes looking down into one's own-those eyes in which there was such fire and, at the same time, such a depth of sadness,-one felt as though one wanted nothing else but to lose one's self in their light. Sandy dimly remembered how those eloquent eyes had, at one time, let go two great liquid diamonds, like drops of dew, that had slowly fallen into his fur. He remembered how the woman had then pressed him more lovingly in her arms, and rubbed her cheek against his silky round head.

He had known more about human kindness than most cats do, even in England; and as much about human beings' coddlings as very few cats ever did in the world. But that more-than-feline and more-than-physical bliss in human arms, he had never yet known, and could never forget. **That**-the touch of a woman who was at the same time a cat-lover **and** a dedicated fighter for a more-than human Idea-had no common measure with his former experiences.

So the familiar pleasures became dull, to him, and life **dreary.**

*   *   *

Everyone in the house used to pet him, above all little Elsie, in whose bed he used to sleep, but also Elsie's mother and father and nearly every friend who came to pay them a visit. The ladies would pick him up and stroke him, and those who happened to see him for the first time could not help exclaiming, no sooner he walked into the sitting room: " Oh, Mrs. Harrington, what a splendid cat you have ! " One even added, one day: " You should exhibit him at the coming cat show. Surely he would get a prize."

But Miss. Harrington resented the idea.

" I'd rather him go without one than have him staying three days in a cage, poor Sandy," said she. " Cats are not made to become exhibits-specially not this one 1" And, smoothing down the feline's thick, stripy coat, she asked jokingly: "Isn't it so, my pet ?"

Sandy looked up to her with eyes full of unaccountable sadness and yearning, and rubbed his head against her legs. She stroked him once more and asked him in a soft voice: " Well, my beauty, what is it ? What **do** you want ?" -for it was obvious to her that he wanted **something,** although she could not make out what... or **whom.**

" Miao !" answered the cat, as he glanced back at her with the same strange, sad look. And this meant: " I want the one who stroked me six months ago; the... Two-legged goddess (what else can I call her ? I don't know her name). I want to lie in her arms once more ! " But Mrs. Harrington did not understand the subtleties of feline speech. She interpreted that " Miao ! " to the best of her capacity, and thought it meant: "I want something more to eat. " So she went and gave Sandy an extra saucerful of fish. Sandy was not hungry. He smelt the fish and turned aside. Again he rubbed his head against his mistresses' legs and said "Miao ! " But again Mrs. Harrington could not understand him. Nor could little Elsie, who imagined the cat wanted to be fondled. Sandy loosened himself from the child's embrace, and quietly walked out of the room.

A peculiar feeling of loneliness crept into him. The old as still a warm place to lie by, curled up upon a cushion, on a chair, from which nobody would disturb him. And little Elsie's bed was still as soft and comfortable as ever. But **something** was not the same. The strange woman with ardent dark eyes and long, white, pleasure-rousing hands-the Two-legged goddess-had crossed his life like a shadow. And nothing could, afterwards, be exactly the same. Everything was more or less dreary in the light of the unforgettable hour in Heliodora's arms, or rather in that of the yearning which that hour had left.

*　　　*　　　*

Sometimes, Sandy would dream of **her,** and give out different sorts of mews in his sleep-smothered mews of contentment, when he dreamt he was in her lap, comfortably curled up, wild mews that sounded like mews of anguish, when he dreamt that she had gone away and left him and that he was roaming in search of her.

Kind Mrs. Harrington was at a loss to understand what to make out of those mews. To her, and to little Elsie, who was growing up, as pretty as ever,- they were just the sign that the cat was dreaming. And what do human beings know about cats' dreams ? Half the time, they cannot even interpret their own properly. Mother and daughter often watched their sleeping pet. Little Elsie would put out her arms as though to comfort him, if the occasional mews happened to sound too doleful. But Mrs. Harrington would prevent her and say: " Don't disturb him ! How would you like to be disturbed when you are asleep ?"

" But mummy, he's having a bad dream, I tell you ! " replied the young girl. And she would stroke the cat gently.

Sandy sometimes imagined it was the beloved and never forgotten hand, and felt so happy that he suddenly woke up... soon to fall back into his slumber, as though he wanted to escape the simple, serene, dreary reality; the kind, familiar faces without passion in their eyes; the familiar laps, that were comfortable enough, but not so full of such particular magnetism as felines alone are able to detect; the familiar caresses which, sweet as they were, lacked the undefinable vibrations to which he had once, and once only, responded, as that Two-legged one had held him an hour long, in her arms, and stroked him, on the cold, lonely footpath, on that memorable, cold, lonely November night that Two-legged one who, in him, had loved and caressed everlasting Catdom and who, apart from him and from it, used to love things not merely more-than cat like but more-than-human, things in which, however, be it indirectly, he, the Cat, had his place.

Sandy was really happy-in spite of his dimmer and dimmer, yet, ever-persistent recollections,- only when he was busy picking out the pieces of liver in the portion of mashed liver and bread that Elsie or Mrs. Harrington used to serve out to him three times a day, or... chasing and catching black-beetles in the scullery; or, when he had just come home after Smut- old Miss Tyrell's pitch-black tom, who lived on the third floor,-had given him a proper " thrashing," and chased him right down the stair-case. Otherwise...-by the Big Cat, Lord of Destiny !-life was as dull as dull can be.

And yet it went on for years...

Many things changed in the house and in the neighbourhood-and no doubt also in the wide world beyond-Sandy's beautiful tortoise-shell coloured mother had died of old age, in spite of all the care both the " vet " and the Harringtons had given her; two of his brothers, whom Elsie had insisted on keeping, were now in the house: one white and yellow, one all yellow, but without stripes. And lately, a Two-legged one had brought in yet another cat: a strange thing with blue eyes and la creamy-coloured fur and dark-brown paws, head and tail (a Siamese) whom Sandy did not like. Would to God the creature had only come for a holiday !- for everyone used to make a fuss of him, and leave poor Sandy to feel lonelier than ever. Mrs. Harrington had even hit her old pet with the back of her hand-not too hard, admittedly; but it was the humiliation, not the slap, that was so painful-for having deliberately scratched the newcomer's face.

And then, one day, the newcomer went away: the same Two-legged one who had brought him came to fetch him with a basket. He **had**, indeed, only come for a holiday (but why for such a long one ? Sandy wondered. Anyhow, he was pleased the cat had gone). Then Smut got run over by a motor-car. And so did one of the young ginger brothers, a few days later; only the half-white one remained.

Little Elsie was now grown-up,- or seemed so to Sandy, who was not good at detecting how old two-legged creatures could be. Sandy himself was slowly ageing: he was beginning to feel somewhat stiff in the joints, and jumping upon the mantel-piece or upon a shelf, was no longer such an easy job for him: nor was catching black beetles such an exciting pastime as before. Ordered by the rhythm of regular meals and sleep, and dreamy dozing by the fireside in winter, and Elsie's and Mrs. Harrington's occasional caresses, life passed peacefully-but without much interest, not to speak of adventure. Foggier and foggier as years rolled by, and yet, at times, suddenly so vivid, the memory of that hour of bliss in the arms of that strange woman persisted in the cat's nerves.

*   *   *

Then came a time when Sandy had grown too weak to move, and lay upon a cushion, in what had once been his mother's basket,- or upon Elsie's bed, but not unless she would carry him there, for he could no longer jump. And he gradually lost his appetite, and would only lie quietly, his large amber eyes sometimes wide open, as though they were gazing at some dream-scenery, invisible to all save himself, sometimes completely closed. He still purred, when stroked; and that purr used to break kind Mrs. Harrington's heart:

" Poor Sandy," she would say: " he is getting thinner and thinner. It looks as though he won't remain with us for long." And she called for the " vet " . But the " vet " diagnosed " old age," and could do no more.

In November, 1955, exactly ten years after that night of bliss that he never could really forget, Sandy out an unusual mew, and stretched his paws convulsively just as he had twelve years before, on the veranda in Calcutta, in Heliodora's lap. And before Mrs. Harrington had time to lift him up, he was dead. His amber eyes still looked as though they were staring at things invisible.

" My poor, poor Sandy ! " cried Mrs. Harrington. And she wept. And so did Elsie, who had now become a beautiful damsel of sixteen springs. Even Mr. Harrington's eyes grew moist as he helped to bury the cat's body in the tiny courtyard behind house, which they called " the garden" But Sandy's soul, which was Long-whiskers' soul and that of so many other cats (nay, that of millions of other creatures in the infinity of times bygone), went and wandered there where souls await their destiny.

. . . an enormous, ginger-coloured cat—Sandy!

CHAPTER IX.

SANDY'S CHOICE

Cats do not know any more about death, and what might or might not come afterwards, than human beings do. The only difference is that most men and women work themselves into believing that they have an opinion concerning this mysterious matter, where cats generally do not bother their glossy heads about it at all. Maybe particularly wise felines do have some sort of hazy intuition of a link between now and tomorrow and some vague feeling concerning their souls, in other words, concerning themselves beyond their last breath. It is difficult for us to assert whether they have or not, as they cannot speak, and as we can neither detect nor even conceive such feelings apart from their expression through speech.

At any rate, it would seem that Sandy was one of those privileged cats, if such there be. For he retained to the very end that one burning desire and that one hope against all hope which had sustained him, in doubtless comfort but actual dreariness, throughout the ten long years that now stretched between him and the great event of his life. And, strange as this may seem, the yearning, instead of continuing to grow vaguer and feebler, became at once more precise and more intense, as death drew nigh. As the cat felt his convulsive paws growing colder and heavier every second, nothing more existed for him but one longing which, translated into human speech, could have been summed up: " Oh, to see her again, be it only once ! and to die in her arms ! " (as he had already died, nearly twelve years before). And as he experienced the ice an inertia of death gradually gaining his whole body, and as he struggled until his heart grew cold and still and until his head fell back upon the cushion like a block of stone, he hung on to the memory of the far-gone rapturous hour, now for a fraction of a second,-more vivid than ever: " Oh, ... **Her**. Her once more ! I want **Her**: the everlasting Great Feline Mother in human disguise; the Two-legged goddess ! " This desperate yearning expressed the last spark of consciousness in the poor dying beast; the last glaring ray of light that crossed his hardening brain, even though his heart had ceased beating.

And as the subtler, interpenetrating, invisible selves left the stone-like body, they retained that active spark, and it kept them together, and it guided their wandering aggregate- what one would call Sandy's **soul**- along the way of its destiny; for desire is the ferment which maintains that differentiation that is at the root of individual life and causes birth and rebirth (even some of the Two-legged ones know **that)**.

*   *   *

Precisely because of that yearning after her whom he too called "the Two-legged goddess ", it had, to the very end, seemed to Sandy as though he could not **really** die; as the mysterious link between moment and morrow **had** to remain unbroken, be it only to allow him to fulfil that overwhelming, unconditional total longing. And so did it remain. And Sandy - or what had worn the flesh and bones and splendid yellow stripy fur that people called " Sandy "- knew that " life continued "

It was, to begin with, a strange experience for him to feel himself **outside** his own body, floating above it, looking down upon it, as though it had not been " his ". It was not the first time, of course, but perhaps the millionth or perhaps the milliardth. But, as creatures' memories are extremely short-confined to one birth only,- it seemed to him strange, utterly strange, as though it had been the first time.

The new state of existence had its advantages, one of which consisted in being able to move with extraordinary speed, without being hampered by such obstacles as walls and closed doors, so that one could go straight wherever one wanted to. Sandy wanted to see the " Two-legged goddess " again; and, curiously enough, in the wink of an eye, there he was, above her bed, gazing at her asleep. He had travelled all the way from Landon to Germany- where she was without even noticing it, as light (and thought) travel. He was there, with her, on her pillow, while the yellow, furry body, that had

84

up till then been his, still lay motionless and heavy, in the same place, in Elsie Harrington's room. He would have liked to rub his head against Heliodora's sleeping face, and nestle comfortably at her side, and have her stroke him,- as on **that** night. But he had forgotten that he no longer **had** any head to rub; nor any to curl up as a ball of fur, upon the sleeper's arm. The new state of existence had also its inconveniences, one of which was that it allowed no further contact with such gross matter as physical bodies are made of.

Sandy, or rather the subtle creature that had been Sandy and Long-whiskers, and many thousands of cats before them, longed to make the woman feel his presence; he longed to, with all his might; he tried to purr-and did, in fact; but it was a subtle, unearthly, dream-like purr that he produced; a purr that no cat and no human being could hear, unless he or she were tuned to the finer Realm. And yet Heliodora's heard it distinctly, and even felt upon her cheek like the touch of a thick, warm, cat's fur. And she woke up at the familiar sensation, and got up to see whether the beautiful black and white cat she then possessed had not come in from his nightly wandering, and greeted her in his own fashion, as he often used to do. But no: there was no cat to be seen anywhere. The black and white one hail come in, but was fast asleep in the depth of the eiderdown. It was not he that had touched her face with his furry head and purred so lovingly. Which cat could it be ?

The disincarnated feline saw the large dark eyes that had poured their love into his, on **that** night. He saw them glance from place to place in search of him, without being able to give further signs of his presence. He knew that, had he but been endowed with a visible body, the woman would have pulled him to her breast, and coddled him, and stroked him, and put her lips to his silky forehead. And he longed for a body of flesh and bones, and fur; a body that other material bodies could touch,- for the abyss between subtler matter and gross matter (he had just found out, for the millionth time) is practically unbreachable.

And as time passed, the longing became more and more intense. It was bound to lead to Sandy's rebirth as another cat. But where ? And under which circumstances ? And with what a destiny ?

*   *   *

"I want to feel myself once more lying in her arms nothing else'"

"And you are prepared to suffer for that privilege ?-for nothing is for nothing, and suffering is the price. "

" I am ready to suffer,-to suffer **anything**- provided I can lie in her arms for five minutes..."

Is such a dialogue but the expression, in human speech, of a struggle within the cat-soul that had been Sandy's and Long-whiskers' and that of many more cats ? Or did it actually take place,-as some saintly cats would doubtless maintain, if they could speak-between that same cat-soul and He-and-She: the Great Tom Cat and the Great Feline other, two and yet One;-Lord and Lady of all being, Master and Mistress of the Spark of Life ? This question is too deep and difficult for Two-legged creatures to answer. But one thing is certain, and that is that, on the twenty-first of January 1957, who Heliodora was admiring an exceptional, blood-red **aurora borealis** in the sky above her little house in Oberricklingen, near Hanover, Sandy-Long-whiskers-was reborn as a tabby kitten, in a miserable back-yard in Teheran.

The invisible Powers of Life had answered his yearning

PART IIII

TABBY
AND OTHER

CHAPTER X.

BLACK VELVET.

Heliodora could no more forget the animal, and especially the cats, that had come into her life, than Sandy had been able to forget her. There was, of course, a great difference: she had been the great event in Sandy's life, as in Long-whisker's, and in Sadhu's, and in that of so many other cats (and dogs) that she had saved from misery- In her life, the great thing was the struggle for the defence of the Third German Reich and, beyond the Reich, for the defence of Aryan man. It exceeded by far the boundaries of the feline world, however much she loved the latter. And yet... One would not remain in keeping with actual facts, were one not to point out what an enormous part animals had played in the shaping of the woman's whole outlook: her love for them had been - coupled with her natural propensity to go to extremes the main origin of her wholehearted acceptance of the National Socialist values **as well as of the methods** which the enemies of the regime called " inhuman ". It had, first and foremost, been her main protection against every sort of anti-Nazi and even- long before the nineteen thirties, during the **First** World War,- against every sort of anti-German propaganda. When people had told her, as a child, that the Germans were " monsters " who used to " chop off children's hands," she had simply answered that it " served the children right "-for she had seen many of them tormenting living creatures, specially insects, or pinning live butterflies upon pieces of cardboard. Her early knowledge of the horrors of vivisection and, even before that, the everyday sight of quarters of meat hanging before butchers' shops, had set her definitely against any exaltation of " man " and the " rights of the human person " and made her indifferent, nay, ostentatiously, provocatively indifferent, to any tortures inflicted upon what she called " two-legged mammals," save when these happened to people she particularly admired, individually or collectively, mostly people who shared her ideas.

Not only had she never felt the slightest sympathy for the " poor Jews " and other alleged "victims of Nazi tyranny, " as we have already stated in the beginning of this story, but she had, from the very start, taken pride in proclaiming to whomever cared to hear her, that this attitude of hers did not proceed merely from the fact that she considered Jews as a dangerous lot. She admitted that, taken individually, they were not all necessarily dangerous, - unless one believed (as she in fact did) in the power of thought, in which case every anti-Nazi, even the apparently most harmless, was to be considered dangerous. And yet, she had no sympathy for them. And she told people so. It pleased her to fling into their faces that boisterous denial of human solidarity, as a life-long protest against man's almost universal indifference to the daily crimes against **life** perpetrated all over the world by slaughterers, trappers, hunters, circus-men and vivisectors.

" As long as the thought of slaughter-houses and vivisection chambers does not keep you awake all night, " she told whomever cared to speak to her, " concentration camps and 'Gestapo methods' of cross-examination shall not disturb **me**-on the contrary ! "

And when some interlocutor would dare point out that " the victims, here, were human beings," she would merely answer: "Of course. And why not ? Human beings are, or can become dangerous to our Cause; animals, never." Such was the attitude Heliodora had kept before and throughout the war. After the war, she became, in her bitterness, still more aggressive, more defiant. To every item of post-war anti-Nazi propaganda, she had an answer. To an English woman who had ventured to mention before her Ilse Koch's alleged " lampshades made out of human **skins,** " she replied: " And what ? I'll condescend to listen to you when I hear you have broken the windows of all the fur shops in London, and helped to lynch the fur-traders,-not before ! In that lamp-shade story, the victims,-if they ever existed,-are not said to have been captured just for their skins, as far as I know. "

In Iceland, in Norway, in Sweden, in England, in France, wherever she went, she stood up for the German doctors tried and hanged for having practiced euthanasia upon incurable patients, or for having performed experiments upon inmates of concentration camps. " A world that censures such actions and that, on the other hand, encourages vivisection and glorifies such fellows as Pasteur, does not deserve to live," declared she. And she fully meant whatever she said. She defied " public opinion "-or rather the opinion dictated to the public by newspapers, films and wireless alike, and backed by what she called " the Christian superstition ". Defiance was, in her case, the most obvious consequence of repeated self-assertion. And repeated self-assertion was the only pleasure left to her in the dreary, post-war world; the world of Germany's " re-education "

In Germany itself, she found oral defiance was not enough, and resorted to open counter-propaganda in defence of National Socialism. She would have resorted to direct, violent action against the " re-education," had it been materially possible : nothing short of that could really have expressed all her contempt for them and their " human values." But oral and **written** provocation, several months long, was enough to land her into trouble. On one fine February night, in 1949, she was arrested and ushered into a dark, damp cell, and left there to wait for the sweet will of the authorities and to meditate upon the price one must pay for the pleasure of supporting, with all its implications, a life-centred faith of political import, in a world ruled according to man-centred principles.

*   *   *

Heliodora was quite happy in her dark, damp cell. Never had she indeed been so happy, since the day she had, in Calcutta, heard hopeful news of the war for the last time. Her coming trial was to give her an opportunity of defying, before a real audience, those man-centred principles which he hated, and of glorifying in public the one great Man who, like herself, had placed a beautiful, healthy police-dog high above a degenerate human being.

In the far-away old room in Calcutta, however, the room with the broad, sunny verandah, full of green plants, thirteen-year-old Sadhu, the last of her cats, was dying -dying of feline distemper, as so many cats do, in India; dying also of dreariness, of loneliness, now that his companion, Lalu, had gone, two years before, never to come back; dying of despair, after having waited some three and-a-half years for that which his poor ageing cat's head could not clearly define, but which his whole being longed for: the old, loving presence about the room; the old lap, in which he used to lie and purr; the hands that used to smooth down his glossy coat; **her**-the " Two-legged goddess ". The friend in whose care she had left him was kind to him: he used to feed him; and stroke him, occasionally. But it was not the same as " her " caresses. So poor Sadhu died- as Sandy was to die some years later- with the persistent yearning for her. And his loving cat-soul came and tried to make her feel its presence in the dark cell. She was too absorbed by other thoughts to become aware of anything such as a furry contact or a purr, but she **did** suddenly think of the cats she had left in Calcutta, and in particular of Sadhu. " Where can they be, now ?" she thought. " And where can he be?" She imagined him basking in the sunshine, on the verandah, with Lalu, of whose loss nobody had informed her. And something told her that she would never see either- or, in fact, any,- of them again.

Several months later, in jail, it so happened that she was, after a search in her cell, brought before the British governor of the prison who- to her utmost pleasure and pride- declared her to be " the most objectionable type of Nazi " he " had ever come across ". Had she remained " natural ", she would have turned to him a beaming face - for this was, in her eyes, the greatest compliment an opponent could pay her. But she had to " put up a show " in order not to rouse the Governor's anger, for upon **his** decision depended the conservation or destruction of certain papers found in her cell. In order to bring for a second, tears into her own eyes, she thought of Sadhu- not knowing that he was dead.

*   *   *

Time passed...And thanks to the shallowness of the Western Allies, who do not take the hostility of sincere enemies too seriously, when these are poor and powerless, Heliodora was released.

In early 1954, she was living in the outskirts of a little Westphalian town, in a tiny room on the first floor, the window of which opened upon a landscape of bushes and fields. In front of her door ran a passage, at the end of which was the stair-case. Her next-door neighbour generally used to leave her baby's perambulator on the landing.

One evening, as Heliodora came home, she found a young black cat comfortably curled up upon the cushions in the " pram ". She knew her neighbour had no cats, and wondered wherefrom this one had come. She could not help stroking him. He purred in response. She picked him up. He purred louder. She carried him into her room; warmed a little milk for him, which he lapped. She had no meat to give him, as she ate none herself, but she gave him some cheese, which he seemed to enjoy. She examined him as she stroked him. He was a pitch-black young tom, with already powerful paws and a round, tigerish head. On his chest, like on Sadhu's, there was one tiny white spot-the only one on his whole body. He strongly reminded her of Sadhu. " Are you really he, come back to me ?" wonder ed she, as she put a kiss upon his head. (She had been told in a letter, after her release, that Sadhu had died). The loving creature purred, so as to say: " I am;-and I have already spent a short cat's life in search of you. Now I was born again, less than three months ago. And at last, here you are ! Don't abandon me ! Keep me ! Prrr, prrr, prrr … "

Heliodora kept him and called him " Schwarzer Sant " " Black Velvet "-for that is what he was: a supple, black velvet body, with golden eyes. His instinct had told him at once that this two-legged creature wanted him; that **she** was the one he had, all the time, vaguely felt he had been seeking, before, between, and after two deaths at least. He jumped upon the woman's bed and nestled against her body, with his head and two front-paws upon her arm. And he purred himself to sleep as she stroked him

The next day, she bought him some pork liver, which he gulped down greedily. She also put in a corner a big flat tin full of fresh, clean sand, the purpose of which Black Velvet immediately understood. In the afternoon, she left the room. And the cat made himself comfortable upon a cushion by the fire and dozed until she returned. He now knew that he had nothing to fear; that he was her cat and that she would always come back to him never abandon him; never give him away save (if ever necessity be) to a second herself.

*   *   *

And he was not mistaken. In the evening, she came back with another piece of pork liver, and another pint of creamy milk for him: ready to receive him in her arms when he had eaten and drunk; and willing to smooth him down and make him purr. And the following day, and every day that came afterwards, it was the same. Black Velvet, who lived in the passing instant, was supremely happy. And so was Heliodora when she did not happen to think of the future.

Black Velvet loved jumping upon her writing table and lying his whole length, flat upon her papers; and also putting out his paw, and trying to catch her pen when she was writing. She would never turn him down; never show him any sign of impatience. At the most, she would softly pull her paper from under him, in order to continue writing,- and at the same time, pass her long white hand over his fur. Or she would stop writing for a while, and tenderly look into his large yellow eyes, as she once used to into Sadhu's. She did not **know** that he was Sadhu himself, reborn for the second time since his death in Calcutta. But she loved him just as much as if she had known. But she loved him just as much as if she had known. She loved him as she loved all felines, big and small- the creatures she felt herself the most attracted to, **after** her human brothers in faith. (In fact, she was more unconditionally attracted to the former, as, in their case, no ideological considerations were at the root of her love).

*   *   *

One fine winter morning, on the 16th December, 1954, there was a hard knock at the door. Black Velvet, who scented danger, jumped from the bed to the table and from the table to the top of the wardrobe and into an old tin which had once contained some twenty kilos of marmalade, but which

94

now lay empty and useless in that high place, looking over the whole room. The tin was just wide enough to hold Black Velvet, curled into a ball of fur, his legs folded under him. But it was deep; and the cat felt safe at the bottom of it.

From that dark, metallic shelter, he heard his mistress get up, throw a dressing gown over her shoulders, and open the door. Then he heard footsteps upon the floor footsteps that sounded heavy, and many. And the door was closed again. Then there were voices : Heliodora's, and three others: men's voices. Black Velvet was surprised not to hear more than three: from the noise of the footsteps,- to which he was not accustomed- it had seemed to him as though a whole battalion had entered the room.

He listened. Through the resounding walls of his hiding place, the voices reached him, amplified. But they were not **angry** voices; apparently, the newcomers were not intent on doing Heliodora any harm- at least, so it appeared to Black Velvet, from his exalted post of observation.

After a while, the cat decided to look and see for himself what was going on-since it now seemed quite clear that he had been mistaken in presuming danger, and since it was, anyhow, beginning to get too hot in his shelter, at the bottom of which there were old papers. So he raised himself upon his hind-legs, put his front-paws on the border of the tin, and " looked out ",- looked down upon the happenings in the room. There was his mistress in her blue dressing gown, sitting on the bed opposite him; two men were seated, each one on one of the only two chairs, while a third man- a stout, round-headed blond,- was standing in front of the wardrobe, exactly below Black Velvet's jam tin.

The men, who were policemen, were putting questions to **Heliodora**. One of them was pointing to Adolf Hitler's picture upon her night-table,- in fact, to the only picture in the room,- as to a proof that the " ominous reports " - against the woman - the reports describing her as a " dangerous underground fighter for Nazism ",- were all too-accurate. Heliodora was answering with the detachment of those who have nothing to lose: " or course I am **His** disciple ! I have never denied I was. Only... I am not " dangerous ", much as I would like to be : most unfortunately, I have not the slightest power."

From the normal, not unfriendly tone of the voices, Black

Velvet surmised that there could be no objection to his coming down, and curling himself up once more in the depth of the eiderdown- so much more comfortable than the bottom of the jam tin, even lined with newspapers. His usual landing place, when springing from the top of the wardrobe, was Heliodora's writing-table. But now, the stout, blond man's powerful skull provided a convenient intermediary landmark along the downward trajectory. The stately representative of re-educated Germany's coercive forces was suddenly shaken by an altogether unexpected bulk, falling, with strange elasticity, upon his head, and jumping off again, while Heliodora could not repress a fleeting smile.

"Ai, ai ! **Was is das ?**" shouted the man, not even noticing, in his amazement, that the cat, that had been among the papers on the table half a second before, had now leaped onto the eiderdown.

" Nothing but a 'black panther'," replied the unrepenting fighter. " But, " she added knowing that this name was used (symbolically) used to designate S.S. men, " no fear ! It is only a four-legged one ! "

The three men had to admire the magnificent cat, now gracefully nestling in the depth of the feather cushion.

One of them asked Heliodora whether he was hers.

"Yes, of course, "said she.

"And what do you feed him on, that he is so sleek and glossy ?" asked another.

" Pork liver, and milk. He won't touch anything else, " was the reply.

It was an accurate statement, but an undiplomatic one, - for after that Heliodora had all the trouble in the world to convince the three policemen- average men, like policemen generally are, all over the earth- that she was merely telling the truth when she declared not having any other income but the ninety marks which a kind soul used to send her every month from India.

"You could not possibly spend so much money on your cat's food if you only had **that** ! " they told her. And as the truth does not always **sound** true, had great difficulty in believing that she actually fed herself on potatoes and macaroni, and was none the worse for it.

*　　*　　*

After thoroughly searching the little room,-which did not take long,-the three men bade Heliodora follow them in their car. She was to undergo a ten hours' cross-examination. For the first time, Black Velvet was all alone the whole day.

At first, he slept. Then, he sat upon the window-sill, and busied himself watching the landlord's lovely white turtledoves, that stood in a row, on the border of the roof. It was not their beauty that roused his interest, but the atavic propensity of the feline to catch birds. Unfortunately (for him) the window was closed. He could at most follow the doves' movements through the glass-pane, making unusual, quivering noises with his mouth, while his whiskers stood out straight. Then the birds disappeared within their shelter, and there was a change in the quality of daylight: the Sun was getting low. Black Velvet now started watching the street below. It was at such a time, more or less, that she generally used to come and bring him his food. He waited and waited to see her on the opposite footpath, to hear her footsteps in the staircase, and the noise of the key in the key-hole. But he heard nothing. And she did not come.

At nightfall, Black Velvet stirred. Was it **she**, at last ? The door was flung open; but it was not **she.** It was Henny, one of the landlady's daughters, who had come in with a dish of pork liver and a cup full of milk for the cat. Heliodora, before going, had requested her to feed him and left her the keys of the room.

Henny loved Black Velvet. And of all people she was, after Heliodora, the one Black Velvet loved the most. She stooped to pick him up in her arms, and she stroked him until she felt, under the thick, warm, glossy coat, the vibration of a responsive purr. When the cat had eaten his food and drunk his milk, she seated herself upon a chair in the midst of heaps of papers and books-the room was topsy-turvy after the policemen's, search-and for a long time, kept him upon her lap. When he had finally purred himself to sleep, she softly placed him upon the eiderdown, and discreetly went away.

He was still fast asleep when Heliodora came back, at 10 p.m. or so. She put down another saucer full of liver the rest kept for him in her " fridge "- and went straight to him. She did not pick him up, not wanting to disturb him. But she lay her cheek upon his fur,- deep down, in the warmth of the eiderdown, where he had curled himself up,- and stroked him. Slowly, from the soft, living cushion, rose a purr; then, the golden eyes half-opened, gazed lovingly into her black eyes, and closed themselves again, while a velvet paw stretched towards her, drawing its claws in and out, rhythmically. Then the whole cushion moved into a new position- head upside down, and front-paws across the chin- and the purr became more subdued and more regular. Now that he knew she was back, now that he had seen her and felt her, Black Velvet could safely sink into the delight of a peaceful sleep. He had nothing to fear. For him, life would continue as before.

*   *   *

It continued: in the eiderdown (or in Heliodora's lap, when she was home) practically the whole day long; In the vastness of the world beyond house and street- over expanses covered with snow, or, soon, with grass and flowers, or growing corn; in the mysterious shade of hedge and bush; up tree-trunks and, occasionally, up some smooth, vertical, telegraph post, from the top of which Black Velvet mewed and mewed before he could make up his mind to come down again- all night, till four or five in the morning.

Heliodora used to write at night, as evening was calm and quiet, and congenial to thought,- but she would interrupt her work once, twice, or more, and go down into the garden behind the house, and often into the field beyond the garden, to see what Black Velvet was doing. She would call him. But he was far too happy, frolicking in the moonlight, to wish to come so soon. He would merely rush towards her, until he was within her sight and then give out a strange mew, as though to say " Here I am ! " and rush back into freedom; or he would lie down some-where,- be it in the shadow of a huge cabbage, be it on the branch of some tree-and look at her mischievously, but not stir. At last,-when daybreak was drawing nigh, and she would come for the third or fourth time, he would run to her,

98

climb up her body, and seat himself upon her shoulders for her to carry him home. There, after eating the food she had cooked for him, he would wait till she had put out the light and gone to bed, and jump up, and work himself into the warm nest, under the quilts, and lie at her side, purring and purring. And he would place his icy-cold paws one after the other into her loving hands, for her to hold them and warm them.

He was as happy as he could be, and his mistress also to the extent there still could be any " happiness" for her after the disaster of 1945.

Then came a change: the landlord needed Heliodora's little room, and asked her to leave. She found nobody willing to lodge her **with** Black Velvet and was thus compelled to **part** from him. But she would at least give him as good a home as she possibly could. She wrote to all the cat lovers she could think of, in and outside Germany, and waited anxiously for their suggestions. The best reply came from an old friend of hers, who lived in the centre of France, who had a garden, and who was prepared to take charge of Black Velvet completely, in case of need. Heliodora knew that nowhere on earth her pet would be as well loved and eared for as in that woman's home. So she lay the cat upon a cushion, in a basket more than big enough for him, and carried him to France. It broke her heart to leave the little room where she had been living so happily with him, for over two years, and the peaceful little township to which she had become accustomed. But there was nothing else she could do.

And thus,-after a long train journey, during which he was " as good as gold "- Black Velvet became the finest tom-cat in a lovely French village nearly three thousand feet above sea-level, surrounded with fragrant fir-tree woods. After entrusting him to the kind friend who was henceforth to take care of him, Heliodora stooped down before the bed upon which he had stretched himself as naturally as if he had known the house for years. She put her arms round him, and kissed his black, soft, thick fur. He purred in response, as he always had. And she, with tears in her eyes,-yet, released, at heart, knowing she was leaving her pet in good hands,- went back to the land of her dreams; the land of her comrades and superiors who were keeping alive the Flame of National Socialist faith, and who would one day (she hoped), seize power once more and rule the West.

She did not know she was never to hold Black Velvet in her arms again.

MIU
"Poor, beautiful cat! How could anyone not love him?"

Heliodora and Black Velvet

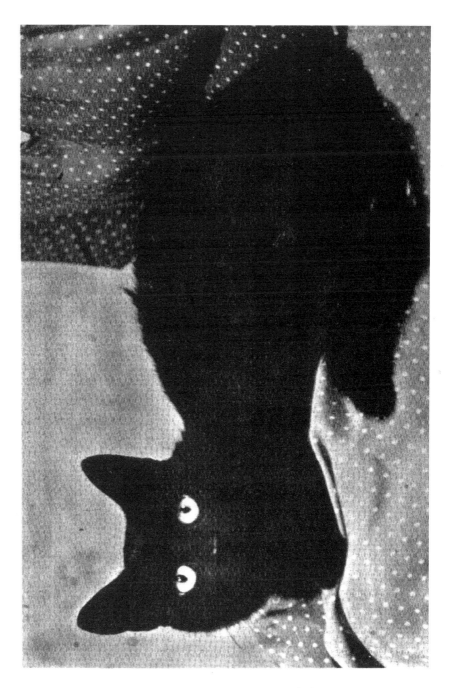

"Nothing but a 'black panther'"

CHAPTER XI.

THE HOUSE IN THE WOODS.

Heliodora went and lived in a garden-house amidst the woods, not far from Hanover, where she had, at last, secured herself a job.

It was a lovely little house; two rooms and a verandah. Through the open windows came, in the spring, the fragrance of lilacs and of fir-trees. The place was silent, save for occasional children's laughter along the narrow grassy path that led from the main road to other garden-houses further within the thicket. There were no radios and no gramophones within audible distance,-and no loud speaking people either. And therefore Heliodora was happy; outside her working hours, she could look into her own soul; think, and write. Sometimes, on Sundays, she would hear a friendly voice calling her by her name, and would rush to the garden gate. And there would stand Herr and Frau S. or one of their daughters, come to ask her to spend the late afternoon with them, in the good old atmosphere she loved-the one she had feared she would never again find in Germany, until... she had come to live there and seen for herself. Now and then, she thought of Black Velvet, and felt sad she had not heard of this garden-house earlier, and been able to bring him with her, straight away. But she had good news of him, and realised how thoroughly he had become accustomed to his second home, in France. She did not want to go and uproot him once more. Nor did she think of taking another cat, for she knew she would one day have to undertake a long journey- for there were things that one could not do, in post-war Europe, specially in post-war Germany, and that she felt it her duty to do. She contented herself warming a bowl of milk and some fish upon her window sill for any wandering cats that might care to come at night. And she soon was glad to see that the food was no longer there in the morning.

And thus days passed, filled partly with her professional work-teaching languages,-to earn her living, and her **real work**: work for the holy Cause, and (whenever she could) for beautiful four-legged creatures.

*   *   *

One morning, as she was closing the door of her room - and making haste, so as not to miss the bus and have to wait half an hour for the next one-Heliodora saw a woman standing before the garden gate, with a cat in her arms.

She hurriedly walked towards her, feeling somewhat anxious (what could be the matter with that cat ?).

" I am sorry to disturb you," said the woman-whom Heliodora had perhaps seen before, but never yet spoken to;- " I was wondering whether you could not find a home for this cat. It is used to being loved and well caped for, and wants a really good home. Its mistress, who lives in that two-storeyed house round the corner, would be glad to keep it, but her husband will have it no longer because it went and did its business... in his shoes ! He threatens to have it destroyed if he sees it in the house again." And she handed the cat over to Heliodora through the bars of the gate.

It was a more-than-half-grown, lovely black and white tom-cat, much like poor Long-whiskers had once been. As soon as he was in Heliodora's arms, he felt himself absolutely secure: he knew no harm could ever happen to him as long as he lay there. And he started a long purr as she stroked his glossy coat, and kissed him on the head, between his short, velvety ears.

" Poor puss !" whispered the Friend of Felines,- the one the starving cats of India used to call " the Two-Legged goddess "- I'll keep you, since nobody wants you; since your own mistress hasn't the guts to stick up for you ! "

And turning to the woman who had brought the cat:

" How utterly senseless ! " said she. " Surely they had forgotten to change his saw-dust. Cats hate using a dirty pan. Fancy threatening to get rid of such a beautiful creature **for that !** " And she added, referring to the cat's former mistress:

" I would have taken the cat with me and left that fellow straight away, and for good, after such a threat ! " She was shivering with indignation.

"Frau P. has three young children," replied the woman. "You are

108

right: that makes things more difficult" admitted Heliodora.

" Anyhow, I thank you for coming to me: I'll keep the cat."

" Frau P. said you would: that is why I came. Mind you: it is not that her husband is so bad as all that; maybe, he would have cooled down and forgotten all about the incident. But one never knows. Frau P. was afraid. Now she will feel released. Oh dear, how released she will feel !"

Heliodora wanted to take leave of the woman. She would miss the next bus as she had already missed the first. Yet, something prompted her to make an enquiry. "Tell me," said she, " by the way: what work does Frau P.'s husband do ?"

" What work he does ? ... But he **does** not work. Don't you know ? "

"No, I don't. What do they live on, then, if he does not work?"

The neighbour put her face against the railing and whispered: " Don't you know ? He had done something in the Hitler days and landed himself in a concentration camp for several years; so now he has a government pension as a " victim of Nazi tyranny," and never was so well off. !"

Heliodora repressed an impulse to say something bitter and perhaps rash. She cast down her eyes and continued stroking the cat, so that the woman might not notice the expression upon her face. She put her a last question, however:

" And you really don't know what he had done ?" asked she. " Something political, surely, for him to be looked upon, to-day, as that which you said. " " Not necessarily. Anyone who has been interned in a camp is a 'victim of Nazi tyranny,' nowadays. In fact, in his case, it was **not** something 'political' if I remember well. It was, I believe, some forgery. Of course, he was **also** against the regime, but that had nothing to do with his trial whatsoever. "

And she quickly put in, as though to " explain " the whole shadowy business to herself and to whomever cared to accept the explanation:

" He is half Czech, anyhow. "

Heliodora bade her good-bye and went back to her house to give the cat some milk (she had nothing else) and shut him in until she would return, in the evening. She then ran to catch her bus.

*   *

When she came back, the cat was sitting behind the window-pane, waiting for her. He rubbed himself against her legs, purring, as she came in,-and purred louder still when he smelt the fish she had brought for him.

She lit the fire and cooked the food, and he ate greedily Then, as she settled down to her writing work, he jumped upon the table among her papers, rubbed his beautiful head against her cheek and said: " Miao !-I want you to caress me. I know you love us felines: I knew it at your first touch, by the way you held me. Miao ! Now I want to lie in your lap while you stroke my fur. See how lovely I am ! Miao ! Your writing can wait… "

Heliodora might not have understood the cat-speech. But she understood the gestures: the movement of the glossy head that pushed itself against her cheek, and purred so invitingly. She pulled her chair backwards, so as to leave enough space for the cat to step down from the table into her lap, and softly said: " Come, my silky tiger ! Come, my purring velvet ! "

How many times had she not uttered those words,- or similar ones-ever since the far-gone day she had, for the first time, held a fluffy black kitten in her arms, when she was two or perhaps less than two, and carried it home, while her mother had kept on telling her: " Be very careful not to hurt him ! Hold him gently ! " How many times had she not let her cheek rest upon a cat's supple body, and enjoyed the feeling of the thick, warm coat, and the regular vibration of the purr, against her skin !

There had been times when she had not been able to keep a cat; times during which her own life had been too unstable, too precarious for her to dare take charge of any creature for the duration of its existence. Such periods that had sometimes extended over years, appeared to her as particularly gloomy, whichever might have been their pleasant features in other respects. In fact, she dreaded their return. And she took to wondering what she would do with **this** cat of hers a year or so later, when she would have to travel, perhaps a long distance, to find someone willing to print her writings. But the cat had nestled in her lap and was softly purring himself to sleep- absolutely unaware of her

110

problems. She stroked the electric fur, as thick and glossy as plush, and a louder purr was the answer to her touch.

She worked at her writing-table, every evening, as before, while the cat slept. Every time she would let her hand rest upon him, the same purr arose out of the living furry cushion. Once or twice the " cushion " would move: turn its head right upside down, and surround it with a large velvet paw- or with **two** large velvet paws, quaintly crossed in a gesture familiar to all felines. Heliodora admired the creature's confidence. " He is accustomed to be loved and knows I shall love him, too," thought she. " Poor, beautiful cat ! How could anyone **not** love him ? In fact, all creatures have that same confidence in man's kindness until they learn, through bitter-sometimes atrocious experience, what a treacherous beast the two-legged mammal often is." Suddenly, in a flash, she recalled the brown dog she had seen in France, years and years before, tied with a chain to the handle of a door in a room of the Science Section of the Lyons University, waiting to be handed over to some vivisector. She recalled the friendly expression in that dog's face; the way he had wagged his tail and tried to leap towards her. He, too, had had confidence in man. - until torture had actually begun at the monster's hands. She recalled her own poor indignation; her curse on all men whose hearts the sufferings of dumb beasts do not move : " A so-called civilisation that takes experiments upon animals as a matter of course deserves to be wiped out. May I see this one blown to pieces within my lifetime !" She recalled the fact that vivisection had been abolished at Adolf Hitler's orders, and pictured herself the German army, the victorious army of glorious '40'marching towards her native town, and the honors that had all her life filled her with hatred for man ceasing at the command of those forerunners of a Fuhrer, better humanity- of the only humanity that she co respect. And tears came to her eyes at the idea that those builders of the world of her dreams had been defeated (and the materialisation of her dreams postponed) through the power of Jewish money.

The cat, who was be beginning to feel too hot in her lap got up, stretched himself, jumped upon the table and lay himself down flat in the midst of Heliodora's papers. She had stopped writing. She stroked him without interpreting the course of her reflections. His silky coat was that of every beast, his loving eyes, the eyes of all life, fixed upon man : ready, at every new generation, to forget the past in the expectation of a new Golden Age-a world in which man no longer would be " the enemy ": the senseless exploiter, the killer, the torturer of all living, beings. At the further side of the table, against the wall was a portrait of Adolf Hitler. And Heliodora's gaze went from the purring feline, lazily stretched upon her manuscript, to the stern and tragic Face of him whom every word of her writing justified and exalted. " O, my hallowed Leader," thought she, " many, so many even among the best of my brothers in faith don't know- should not understand-the secret of my allegiance to **You** and to the German Reich. But you would have understood, had I been able to approach you; I am sure you would have... I hail in you, my Leader, the Avenger of Creatures : the One who treated hated man as he treats them; the Chosen One of divine retribution, Sword of Justice, Whom Life had been awaiting millions and millions of years ! Of all the nations of the world that condone cruelty to dumb beasts " in the interest of man," every one is as bad as the other, and there is not one of them that I should not gladly betray and destroy, if I could. But, oh my sacred Third German Reich, for you whose laws put a full stop to the agony of vivisected beasts, and for you alone,- for your resurrection, now that the evil Forces have won for the time being, - I live, and should be glad to die. May I see your armies of liberation again overrun the world ! I never did care, and still don't care, how your enemies were treated. They had never raised their voices in favour of the dumb creatures tortured in the name of criminal curiosity, gluttony or sport. Why should **I** raise my voice in their favour ? Nothing bad enough could happen to them, since they stood in your way. "

*   *   *

It was late when Heliodora retired. The cat followed her into the neat little room and jumped upon the bed, quite sure she would not turn him off.

The fire had gone out. It was cold. The woman stroked the

cat that had curled up in the depth of the eiderdown - just as Black Velvet once used to do. But soon she lifted the blankets for him to be able to get inside, if he cared to. And she called him as she did so : " Come, my puss ! Come, my dark tiger ! "And he understood the inviting voice and stepped in, and lay down against her, purring as she continued to stroke him. He finally went to sleep, his round, glossy head resting upon her shoulder, and one paw stretched out upon the pillow.

Days passed-and weeks. Heliodora and her cat which she had started calling " Miu,"-were happy. Miu had forgotten his former mistress. Heliodora never forgot Black Velvet. But she had excellent news of him: after a period of extensive wanderings, during which he had been busy pursuing the she-cats of all the neighbouring hamlets, he had settled down in his new home and become as sleek as ever before. His coat, in the harsh climate of the mountain village, had become extraordinarily thick. And because of that good news, Heliodora did not regret having taken him there. And she loved Miu as much as she continued to love him-as much, in fact, as she loved all cats, nay, all felines.

For thus was her nature: she did not really love **individuals** of any species,- not even two-legged ones like her own self; not even those whom she admired as " samples of higher humanity ". She caressed the intangible Essence of Catdom- feline grace, mystery, and sensuous affection - in **any** cat, just as she sought, in every healthy, pure-blooded Aryan, and specially in every better type of German or Northern European, her ever-receding ideal of human perfection: the intangible Essence of her own race. She had done so all her life. This was perhaps one of the reasons why she had always felt herself so much more at ease with animals than with most human beings : an animal expresses more faithfully the collective Self of his species than most individual men or women do that of their respective nations or races. And yet, she was deeply conscious of the fact that every individual living creature, man, woman, cat, dog, bird, fish or insect, nay, even every leaf of a tree, is unique and irreplaceable; that the divine collective Soul of the species shines in him, her or it, as it could not, cannot and never shall again be able to, in any other finite body. And that is why, without attaching herself exclusively to any, she considered every individual so earnestly: as a fleeting shimmer upon the ocean of endless Time, and still, a shimmer reflecting Eternity.

And that is how she loved Miu- Catdom at hand; the essence of all felines, including the royal tiger, too far away and too wild to stroke- purring in her arms. Knowing she was one day to part with him, she attached herself to him as though every day had been the last one she was allowed to spend at his side in the peaceful little house in the woods.

*   *   *

Heliodora had a young pupil, a German, little over twenty-two, whom she loved dearly because of his manly beauty, his wisdom, far beyond his years, his unshakable faith in their common Leader, Adolf Hitler, and all he stands for, and... his kindness to animals, especially his solicitude towards cats.

She had discovered him at the language school where she was a teacher. A casual remark of his had sufficed: she had grown accustomed to detecting other National Socialists, comrades of hers, amidst the dumb crowds of people all " uninterested in politics," whom she daily came in touch with. And the young man had started coming to spend his evenings at the little house in the woods-to improve his French, and to talk freely of his grievances against post-war society in general and Dr. Adenauer's government in particular; of his National Socialist convictions, which were also Heliodora's; and of his dreams, less unpractical than hers.

He lived not far away from her, in a room without heating, which was cheap, for he had to save money and finish paying as fast as he could for the tape-recorder that he had bought on credit to repeat his French lessons over and over again. He used to work in an office and take his midday meals on the spot, with the other clerks. In the evenings, he often used to go without a meal. When Heliodora came to know that, she bade him share her supper whenever she herself **had** anything to share.

As soon as she came home from her work, sometimes at 9 p.m., sometimes at 10, she would first light the stove and

114

prepare the cat's food. Miu, who was glad to see that she was back,- and glad to smell the promising fish she had brought him-kept rubbing his head against her legs and purring as loud as he could. Then the sound of a bicycle would be heard along the narrow, dark path, beyond the hedge bordering the garden, and a bell would ring before the gate. Heliodora knew it was her young comrade, for nobody else would ever come so late. And she would let him in, return his " Heil Hitler! " (they never exchanged any other salutation) and nearly always add the words of caution : " Be careful ! Mind the cat does not go out ! "

" Right-quite right," would reply the young man, and close the door speedily, and go and make himself comfortable in a corner of the little room, by the window.

While she was watching the cat's food, so that it might not boil over, he generally asked her something, or told her some news, as for instance : " Did you read the latest issue of **'Der Weg** ' ?" or, " I met Herr S. He gave me an invitation for our next meeting. Naturally, you are coming, aren't you ? "

Heliodora answered without taking her eyes away from her saucepan : " Of course I am ! I'll be a little late, no doubt: I shall be working at the school till nine o'clock. But I'll come. You don't imagine me missing a 9th of November meeting if I can possibly help it, do you ?"

"As for ' **Der Weg** ', I have it here, if you have time to read it. Frau M. has just given it back to me. There is, in it, a heart-rending article about the fate of Mussolini's eagles after the fall of the Fascist regime: how the anti-Fascist mob left them,-one dead, the other more dead than alive- after poking out their eyes, breaking their wings and legs, torturing them in the most abominable fashion, poor royal birds; and how a kind soul, the eagles' former keeper, rescued the living one, blind and maimed, and gave it shelter in his own house until it died, only the other day,-nearly ten years after the scene of torment. It seems that he had taken care of it so well that it had become able to stand once more upon a stick, and that it had grown touchingly attached to him. This article has profoundly upset me. There is nothing so cowardly, nothing so degrading as to take revenge upon a beast. The thought of those eagles, and of the human fiends who tortured them, haunts me. Not that I am in any way astonished to read of our enemies doing such things- it and gave it shelter in his own house until it died, only the other day,- nearly ten years after the scene of torment. It seems that he had taken care of it so well that it had become able to stand once more upon a stick, and that it had grown touchingly attached to him. This article has profoundly upset me. There is nothing so cowardly, nothing so degrading as to take revenge upon a beast. The thought of those eagles, and of the human fiends who tortured them, haunts me. Not that I am in any way astonished to read of our enemies doing such things- it is not the first time I hear of similar atrocities. Yet, they always haunt me... One thing is at least certain : none of **us** could ever commit such crimes as those "

" I should think not !" exclaimed the young National Socialist vehemently.

" I know I am right," said Heliodora. " Once, at Frau W's, I met a man who had himself taken an active part in the well-known ' Kristall Nacht '. We had coffee together. I asked him whether he or any of his comrades had ever molested any cats, dogs or other beasts because they happened to belong to Jews. He told me quite emphatically that neither he nor any of the raiders had ever done anything of the kind, nay, that **they had definite orders to spare and protect dumb creatures. "**

Miu, the cat, after eating his fish, went and jumped into the young man's lap and remained there, curled up, regularly purring, till the end of the evening, as he always used to. And the conversation would continue between Heliodora and her pupil, until the latter would at last leave the house, at about 12 p.m., or sometimes one o'clock in the morning. Apart from his uncompromising National Socialist orthodoxy, the woman admired in him the virtues of the everlasting German soul: patient energy, endless day to day courage, readiness to total sacrifice, warrior-like pride **and** along with that- kindness; a sincere and intelligent love of animals, of trees, of all beautiful, innocent life. She set great hopes upon his youth-she, who was more than twice his age- and imagined him one day playing a leading part in the management of a grand National Socialist Europe; helping to reorganise the whole continent according to her own cherished dreams, when he would be as old as she was then, and she, dead. Gladly she would have accepted to lose a limb if, at that price, through some extraordinary magic, the young man could have become her son.

The cat loved him, too, in his own way, and for his own reasons. There was a sweet, homely atmosphere in the little cottage, by the lamp-side, whenever the three were there together,- a restfulness that Heliodora deeply appreciated, she whose life had been a ceaseless struggle. She sometimes wondered how it was, in spite of all, possible for her to be **so** happy, even then, in that atrocious post-war world, nearly twelve years after the disaster of 1945; so happy, between the handsome and ascetic young idealist who shared her Hitler faith so completely, and little cat, who lay either on his lap or in her arms, and whose voluptuous grace was that of all cats, of all felines,-the divine gracefulness which she valued far more than the alleged " reason " of the vast majority of two-legged mammals.

She knew that the picture of the young man- future Germany- sitting at her working-table, would for ever remain in her memory linked with that of the cat. And she remembered that the hero Horst Wessel had been, he too, a great cat-lover. (His own aunt, Fraulein Richter, had told her so, and even shown her a photograph of him amidst a dozen cats of the neighbourhood).

At night, once his friend had gone, Miu, the splendid black-and-white tom, so like Long-Whiskers, (although he was not he), would often mew at the door, which meant: " **Do** let me out ! It is so lovely to take a stroll in the snow, under the bright moon, shining through the bare tree-tops ...Don't fear : **I'll** come back all right ! "

And Heliodora used to let him out. But, in spite of the bitter cold, she would leave the window partly open lest he should return during her sleep and wait and wait in the snow, without being able to come in. In the very early morning, before dawn, she would generally feel something soft and warm against her cheek, and wake up to see Miu trying to push himself into her bed. She would then slightly lift the blankets and let him in, and hold his icy-cold paws, one after the other, in her hands, to warm them, as she once used to hold Black Velvet's-while he lay purring at her side.

*   *   *

Spring returned, and the little house in the woods as became more delightful than ever. Again lilacs flowers and the old cherry-tree blossomed in the garden, and the whole place was alive with birds' twittering and joyous sunshine and the days grew longer and longer. And there was sunshine so peaceful as the slow twilights.

Whenever Heliodora had not to go out,-whenever she had no lessons at the language school- she would sit in a deckchair before her house, on the verandah, or in the garden among the lilacs, with the cat in her lap, and watch the day gradually fade into darkness. Had she followed her inclination without thinking any further, she would have bought the poor dear cottage (she **could** have: she had saved enough money by now) and remained there for good. The beauty and quietness of the surroundings; the comrades she had in the town nearby and all over Germany, only a few hours' journey away; the devoted young fighter, one of the best of them all, who still used to come regularly and spend nearly every evening with her in fiery evocations of the glorious recent past and of the ever-nearing future, everything tended to retain her. The cat himself, so comfortably curled up in her lap, relaxed, absolutely sure of her love- happy- seemed to tell her, as he softly purred : " Surely you'll never abandon me !"

She did not **want** to part from him- or from her German surroundings and from the German people, to whom she had grown more and more attached.

And yet... there was a call-an irresistible duty or what appeared to her as such-which mercilessly drew her away from all that. She had written a few books and she felt that time had come for her to have them printed, if only to tell her German comrades that, even though the whole world frantically growled abuse against them, **someone** stood, in spite of all, and would always stand on their side and on Adolf Hitler's- on their side precisely because of Adolf Hitler and his Gospel of pan-aryan pride, in keeping with the aristocratic spirit of Nature. But she would have to go far in order to find somebody willing to print such a tribute to the persecuted

Nation and her ever-lasting Leader. No one in Europe would dare to... So she would again have to go to the East-to tolerant India where people don't care and will print anything. The kind old friend who had taken Black Velvet would also take Miu: she had just written, telling Heliodora that she could bring him whenever she pleased.

And so, one evening, the woman finally left.

The fair young man came for the last time to help her carry her things- and the cat-to the railway station, and to see her off. He closed the garden-gate behind her and walked ahead. Holding the travelling-bag at the bottom of which lay Miu, as comfortable as ever and half-asleep, she slowly followed the narrow, grassy path that led to the main road. And then, before leaving it forever, she looked back and gazed at the little house, now empty,- the house she loved, and where she **could have** remained;- at the lilacs, the fragrance of which - she deeply inhaled; at the old cherry-tree whose branches seemed to her as loving arms, stretched out to her in the darkness. And tears welled up to her eyes.

In the train, she kept the bag on her lap. Miu soon put his head out and looked all round him, as though he wondered where he was. Then, as his mistress stroked him as usual, he felt himself in safety, and went to sleep, to the regular noise of the wheels that carried him nearer and nearer to his new home.

120

CHAPTER- XII.

HELL ON EARTH.

" Nothing is for nothing, suffering is the price." And one will remember that, at the time his everlasting Self had left its furry abode and faced the critical moment that was to determine his next birth, Sandy had chosen the way of suffering :- a life of misery for the sake of lying once more, for a few minutes, in the arms of the one he could not forget.

So he came back into the world as one of the five kittens of a poor emaciated mother-cat- an ordinary black-and white street cat, like Long-whisker's mother had once been. But instead of a cow-shed in a Calcutta lane, his birthplace was, this time, a garage at the back of a courtyard in Teheran. He came into the world upon a dirty rag, - the remnant of what had once been a sack -under a motor-car that was standing there, with several others, awaiting repair. He was tabby, with nice, regular stripes, and a better fur than his mother's, for his father was " angora "- or half-angora. He had one black-and-white brother and three sisters : one also black-and-white and two tabby-and-white.

His mother purred as she lay upon the scrap of cloth with her live little ones hanging at her breast. She would lick him from time to time. And for a few hours, perhaps a few days, he was as happy as any newly-born creature could be: it was not so cold inside the garage as out of doors, and not so cold under that car, in the very corner near the wall, as it was elsewhere in the garage; not so cold, also, upon that torn and tattered piece of rag, as upon the bare dusty earth.

At times, generally at night, the mother -at would leave her kittens and go and wander round the refuse-heaps in search of fishes' heads, chicken bones, (or intestines), an occasional bit of meat or skin-any scrap fit to still her hunger - or, when she was lucky, catch a couple of gutter-mice. She used to come back early in the morning to find her little ones crying for her. And she would " talk" to them in soft, subdued little mews-"

Rrrrmiao ! Rrrrmiao ! Rrrrm! Rrrrm ! " -and lick them lovingly as all mother-cats have been doing ever since the origin of catdom. The two-legged creatures that worked in the garage, changing tyres and repairing motor-car engines all day long, did not seem to take any notice of her and of her progeny.

But one day the car under which the little family was rapidly growing was removed. It was in the morning, but the mother that had apparently wandered further than usual in search of food, had not yet come back. The five kittens, huddled against one another in the " bed " in which they had been born, were desperately calling her, in tiny, high-pitched voices. A boy roughly pushed the rag away with his foot, and them with it, as though they had not existed; a lorry came rolling in and placed itself in the empty comer. There was a squeal from one of the baby: cats, a tragic cry of pain immediately drowned in the noise of the engine. Nobody even noticed that a living tabby-and-white ball, a creature of beauty that had opened its large blueish eyes to the daylight less than a fortnight before, had just been crushed under the monstrous tyres.

*   *   *

The mother-cat came back, nursed the four kittens that were left... and days passed. As little young cats grew, they became bolder, and started wandering a yard or two away from their headquarters. The little tabby tom, that had been Sandy and Long-whiskers, was the boldest of the four; he would sometimes wander out of the shady space under motor-cars and lorries, into the open sunshine-and sometimes even across the courtyard into the street. It is true that he had always shamelessly taken more than his share of the little milk the poor mother had been able to give, pushing aside his weaker brother and sisters with all the brutality of a confirmed believer in the rights of the strong in universal struggle for survival. The other unfortunate kittens were half his size.

Nobody seemed to be aware of their presence, or of that of the bold young tom, or of the skeleton-like mother, whose bones jutted out under her thin fur. Nobody fed them, nobody even thought of putting aside, for them, a few; crumbs from one's midday meal. Nobody loved them. But nobody did any positive harm to them until, one day, the owner of the garage- a Jew from Russia who, in 1945,. had fled to Iran for fear of being deported by the Germans; who had become rich within the following six months and embraced Bathaism, or pretended to, for reasons better known to himself,- happened to notice one of the little ones answering the call of nature in a shady passage between two cars. Turning to his Persian manager, he said:

" Those cats are a nuisance. I wish you'd could get rid of them " " Most certainly, " answered the Persian manager, always on the look out to please the boss, as long as this did not imply any inconvenience to himself.

So the next day, one of the apprentices was told to pitch the kittens into a bag and to go and throw them wherever he liked,-" sufficiently far away for them not to come back." The boy found the young tabby's brother and his two remaining sisters, flung them into an old oily duster, and, on his way home, dropped them as a matter of course into a gutter on the aide of the road- to die of hunger and misery after mewing for their mother for days and nights, without a single one of the two-legged passers-by even giving them a thought.

The young tabby tom, however, was not thrown away to die with them, for it happened that he was not there when the others were collected, and that the boy-who had been told to take them **all** away- was too lazy to search for him.

It was later than usual when the mother-cat came back to the garage. She called her little ones as she did every day, in soft, loving mews, again and again, but no kittens' voices **were** heard in reply to hers. The poor baby-cats were calling her- calling her desperately, in hunger and distress, at the bottom of the murky ditch into which the boy had thrown them. They were to keep on calling her all day and all night, and all the next day and following night, till their tiny throats, parched with thirst, could call no longer; till their exhausted bodies grew weaker and weaker... But they were too far away for her to hear them. So she mewed and mewed in vain, pitifully, for a time that seemed endless to her, feeling as one does when one has lost everything.

At last, a faint kitten's mew **did** answer hers– or was it an illusion ? Hope, mixed with anxiety, suddenly filled her heart.

She ran to the place the feeble voice had come from: a narrow space between a huge case full of iron spare parts and the wall; the place into which the tabby kitten rushed for shelter, as one of the workmen, knowing (as they all did, by now), that the boss did not want the cats, had kicked him away from the door-step.

"Rmiao ! Rrrrmiao !" mewed the mother.

" Mee-u ! Mee-u ! Mee-u " answered the baby-cat, as he struggled out of his hiding place the best he could,-and not without difficulty.

The mother-cat licked him, purring for joy. Then she roamed about the garage, sniffing under every car and every lorry, and calling her other little ones from one corner of the place to the other. If she had found **that** one, the others could not be far away, felt she, unaware as she was (in spite of repeated experience) of the senseless cruelty of man. She called them and called them, with growing restlessness, amidst the two-legged creatures, busy with their own affairs, who paid no attention to her or to the kitten running at her side. Even the boy who had thrown away the wretched babies did not seem to hear the mother's mews, as she passed near while, while he was putting a new tyre to a wheel. Or if he heard them, he did not care. He was ignorant, coarse and heartless, as in fact many are, who have gone to school longer than he ever had, and was at most capable of swallowing propaganda about a dream-world in which the poor would divide among themselves the wealth wrung through violence from the rich. He had no feelings for creatures other than human beings, and had not given as much as a thought to the kittens he had flung into the ditch to mew until they would become too weak to utter a sound, and finally to die of hunger. And he would have been amazed, nay indignant, had anybody told him that he well deserved the very fate he had imposed upon them. So the distressed mother-cat went by with her tabby son, thoroughly unnoticed.

The garage manager was the first one to become aware of her presence and of that of the kitten. He was not a hater of cats. Yet, dreading what his boss might say, were he suddenly to turn up and see that his orders had not been strictly carried out, he stamped, and pretended to fling a stone so as to frighten the cats away- out of the garage, across the courtyard and right into the street. There, some despicable children pursued the mother and kitten with actual stones- " for fun "-until they both found shelter behind a pile of empty cardboard boxes, in front of a shop. The shop-keeper chased away the children for having caused one of his boxes to roll into the gutter; and so, the cats were safe- for the time being. Fear kept them in their hiding place as long as there were two-legged ones going up and down the footpath, and in and out the shop. At night, the mother went back to the old garage, mewing, in search of her three lost little ones. All night she mews for them in vain... while they, poor things, were still calling her-in vain, also- at the bottom of the ditch where they were slowly dying. Then, gradually, the haunting feeling of them grew less vivid in her: hunger, and the care of the remaining tabby kitten, that needed her, pushed aside all other worries...

The next day, the two starving beasts managed to fill their bellies with scraps of meat and chicken bones, fished out of a refuse-heap, in the back-yard behind a restaurant. And they slept well-unseen, upon a bundle of dusters, under the counter of the same restaurant. And the kitten hung to his mother's breast, purring, before he fell asleep. These were his last happy hours. On the following day, the mother-cat was killed:- run over by a motor-bicycle as she was trying to cross Takke Avenue in a hurry. She lay all day dead, a streak of blood pouring from her mouth, upon the asphalt of the broad, modern way, under the bright spring sunshine. As usual, nobody seemed to take any more notice of her than if she had been a scrap of paper.

*   *   *

The poor tabby kitten, little over two months old, for whom she had been everything, was now all alone in the wide world.
He had already experienced the pangs of hunger, the occasional brutality of a dog running after him, and the permanent indifference or cruelty of the two-legged mammal. But he had had his mother's love: her purr, in answer to his, when he slowly used to go to sleep at her breast; her soft little mews of love-the only kind voice he knew -calling him,

when he had wandered a few yards too far away; the familiar feeling of her rough tongue against his young fur. Henceforth he was alone in that huge underworld of desperate struggle and of misery: the cat world of Teheran, as far below the human realm and as thoroughly cut off from it as the latter is, itself, below the invisible realm of spirits, good and evil, and incapable of coming in touch with it, save exceptionally.

Poor tabby kitten - that had been proud Long-whiskers, and had once known happiness in Heliodora's heaven like Calcutta home; that had been majestic Sandy and lived twelve years among people who had loved him, and whose life he had shared ! What made things worse was that the River of Oblivion- what the ancient Greeks called Lethe- runs between every life and the same individual's following one, for cats just as for other four-legged or two-legged creatures, therefore that the young tabby tom-kitten **did not know** that it was he himself who had chosen to be reborn into a world of suffering, nor why he had made such a choice. He did not remember the woman who had appeared to him as to so many hundreds of felines and other creatures as the " two-legged goddess " Nay, ever since he had been frightened out of the garage, he had not pictured himself the two-legged mammal as anything else but a cruel giant that one had to run away from, as from the worst type of dogs, which are nearly as nasty.

And yet, how many a child of a nobler and kindlier humanity- a child like little else or, in fact, Heliodora herself, had once been- would have been delighted to hold the young tabby in her arms ! For he was a pretty kitten, with a sweet little round face full of the usual mischievous expression. He had lovely eyes, which had been bluish-grey and were now slowly turning greenish-yellow. And his fur was long and silky, and his velvet paws big for his size, showing that he was to become a powerful tomcat, if only he was allowed to live long enough.

He would have been the finest kitten in the world, had he regularly had enough to eat. And even so, thin but fluffy as he was, he would have been the joy of any lover of feline beauty. The tragedy was that very few of these were ever likely to come across him.

*   *   *

At first, he mewed for his mother, not realising that she had been run over. Then, as he wandered back to the spot and saw her body lying in a pool of blood, it dawned upon him that she would never move again-never purr again; never call him, never feed him, never lick him again. And he mewed, this time out of distress. He felt abandoned. He felt like a child would feel if a car dropped him in a desert place and drove off; or if a ship landed him upon a lonely island and sailed away. " Mee-u ! Mee-u ! " shouted he, as he stood, a tiny dark speck in the midst of broad Takke Avenue. Had a friendly hand come at that moment and taken him up and stroked him, how he would have purred, for sheer joy of experiencing a little love. But no kind person happened to pass that way, or to notice the slender, fluffy spot of life in the vastness of the asphalt desert. Several cars rushed past-one, so near him that the kitten was actually flung off his feet through sheer strength of the wind that the vehicle roused on its way. And before he had time to get up and come to his senses, another huge thing on wheels was following the first, at full speed- this time a lorry, that made a terrific noise. The tiny creature was panic-stricken. He threw himself across the avenue at the risk of his life, and finally found himself projected by a last gush of wind into a ditch.

The place was cool, compared with the asphalt of the avenue; cool and safe. In spite of the noise they made, motor-cars and lorries seemed to roll past far away, over one's head. And one neither saw them nor felt the wind they provoked. The little tabby kitten wandered in what appeared to him as a shady valley, until he discovered a mad leading upwards: a way along which he climbed, over a heap of pebbles and crumbling earth, up to the level ground on one side of the avenue. He found himself at the foot of a hedge and finally,- after he had managed to struggle through the latter,- in an open, grassy expanse: a lawn in the garden surrounding the American Embassy, in which he frolicked about, running after beetles and butterflies until he grew tired. There, too, nobody noticed him: the garden was broad; the gardener was not there that afternoon; and the voices were too far away for anyone who walked in or came out to become aware of his presence.

Then, all of a sudden, the air became cooler. Daylight was different. The Sun was setting. And soon night came; night, with all its stars. And the poor little tabby kitten wandered in that well-kept garden as he once had-fifteen years before-in the back-lanes of Calcutta between Dharmatala Street and Corporation Street, before he got himself, by mistake, shut in that " go-down, " out of which Heliodora had rescued him. But then, he had at least had his mother. Now, he was all alone-and more and more hungry.

He mewed. And just as then, the repeated high-pitched cries of distress- " Mee-u ! Meee-u ! Meeee-u, "- marred the solemn majesty of the starry night. But this time there was nobody to hear them. The one who had come, then, in answer to his despair, was now some five thousand miles away. She would come, but not yet. " Nothing is for nothing; and suffering is the price. " Such is the decree of an implacable and universal Destiny; the law of Creation. For the poor tabby kitten, a life of suffering had begun. It was to become worse and worse until the end... and the long-forgotten reward.

*   *   *

Until the day before, he had often known hunger. But he had had his mother's love. When the thin, miserable she-cat that she was had no milk, still she would lick him; still she would " talk " to him in such undertones, caressing little mews that he used to feel protected, nearly happy, in spite of all. Now he was hungry and had no mother's love. He mewed and mewed till the 'first light of dawn; till his little throat was sore. Then, he fell asleep out of sheer exhaustion... only to wake up suddenly, two or three hours later, completely drenched-for the gardener watering the lawn had not seen him; or not cared, and directed the jet of his hose right upon him.

The kitten got up, terrified, and ran away as fast as he could, out of the wide-open gate and across Takke Avenue, where his mother still lay dead. Traffic was not so intense, then, as later on in the morning, so no accident happened to him before he reached Roosevelt Avenue, just opposite the Greek Orthodox Church. But from some courtyard near that church, he then heard a dog bark. And although the sound came from so far away that, reasonably speaking, he had nothing to fear, he ran faster... until he found a passage- the narrow space between the side-wall of a house and some big case full of rubbish that was there, before it- to rush and hide into.

There he remained long hours, hungry, but too afraid of the thousand-and-one unusual shapes that he saw passing by, and of the various sounds that reached him, to dare put his nose out. In the end, however, as evening came, the persistent smell of roasted meat that the breeze brought to him from a neighbouring restaurant, incited him to muster his courage and walk towards the place, for he was by nature carnivorous, as all felines. For his good luck, just at that moment, a customer who was eating inside the shop a portion of chicken with some rice flung on to the footpath a bone with a little flesh and a long bit of skin hanging from it. The kitten rushed and picked it up, and, after taking it to his secret " corridor " between case and wall freely ate the skin and whatever scraps of flesh he could find to gnaw. But as he came out once more, and hesitatingly made for the entrance of the shop from which the smell of food was coming a nasty child threw a stone at him. Quickly, the poor kitten ran back to his precarious shelter, and remained there too frightened even to thrust his head forwards.

At night, as the pangs of hunger became more and more unbearable, he cautiously crept along the wall and finally into the shop, the door of which was still open, and managed to eat a few scraps: bits of skin and bits of half meat fallen from the customers' tables, and an occasional bit of soft bread that he took a long time to chew with his sharp, but tiny little newly-grown teeth. He fell asleep at last under a stool in a corner, where nobody had noticed him.

But the next morning, as he woke up and started walking about, a servant stamped and shouted (as the garage manager had once done) and chased him away. He ran to his former hiding place, behind the case in the side-street. But it was, alas, no longer there:- the case had been removed. The poor kitten looked up pitifully and utter a feeble mew: a mew of distress; the mew of a baby-cat abandoned among men. Then, he followed the wall. Where to ? He did not know. He only knew- and that was the result of his first two days of lonely struggle -that the foot of the wall was, after the gutter, the least dangerous place in the street. The gutter being, then, full of water, he followed the wall. He had began that awful life which is that of all stray animals in the towns and villages of the East; that hellish life which very few cats indeed are able to endure to an advanced age.

He wandered and wandered: to the junction of Roosevelt Avenue and of the next great artery of Teheran: and along the latter, to the right, for fear of crossing it. He wandered and wandered, and did not find anything to eat apart from a spoonful of rice-pudding that he discovered near the foot of a customer's chair, in front of a tea-shop. And when his legs were unable to carry him any longer, he lay down upon a heap of planks, in a courtyard into which he had rushed for shelter, to avoid falling into the hands of some cruel children, and **slept like a log.** The following morning he was abruptly thrown- still asleep from his plank on to the hard cement floor, and woke up as in a bad dream, feeling sore from top to toe. Limping, and more hungry than ever, again he wandered and wandered, finally coming back to the crossing of Roosevelt Avenue, where he had been two days before- thus roughly fixing the limits of the area where as henceforth to be " his, " i.e., over which he was to wander for the rest of his life (save if exceptional events forced him to change his habits) and every nook and corner of which he was to get acquainted with.

*   *   *

Days passed. Weeks and weeks passed. In spite of terrible hardships- permanent hunger, fear and misery, and occasional human cruelty- the tabby kitten grew. And he quickly learnt from experience a few useful things: **first**, that it is preferable to be out at night than in the daytime, if one possibly can: for not only is it, then, easier to hunt for food, but one does not come across so many two-legged creatures, most of which are devils that throw stones at one, or water (nay, sometimes boiling water) or dust (that gets into one's eyes) when they happen to very young and not strong enough to throw anything else; **second** that, notwithstanding the better scraps that one sometimes finds there, one should avoid places where two-legged creatures are seated: one runs the risk, there, of getting kicked, or perhaps even crushed. If one spots on the floor anything that really looks appetising, one should rush and snatch it away in the wink of an eye, and go and eat it in a safe corner- not among the tables and chairs and two-legged creatures' feet, where the worst may occur. **Third**, that it is advisable never to go into the places in which the two-legged creatures prepare food. One **might** of course, have there the exceptional good luck of getting at a really big and fresh chunk of meat, or of lapping up any amount of milk, undisturbed, provided one creeps in when the place is empty and takes care not to stay there too long. But it is very risky; dangerous, one should say. One can never tell what the monsters might do if they catch one before a saucepan of milk, a joint of meat, or even a heap of poultry intestines (which, by the way, they **don't** eat themselves). It is much safer to go, at night, and scratch and sniffle into the malodorous hillocks (generally twice or three times as high as an average cat) that are to be found along the streets, sometimes in courtyards, or into the bins, also full of foul smelling refuse, that most of the time stand nearby. In the beginning, one has, of course, to overcome the nauseating smell of decaying vegetables, flesh and fish. But one grows less sensitive to it, bit by bit. And in the end, when one has not had anything to eat for three days, and can find nothing else, one is glad to pull a knot of chicken's entrails of the day before, from under a disgusting heap of ashes, curds gone sour, bones, and half-putrid rice and vegetables. It stills one's hunger; it is better than nothing at all !

And finally... avoid those big, noisy box-like things that move about on four or two wheels; those that purr, but much louder than cats, and in a vulgar, ostentatious manner, releasing la breath that stinks like poison. And...avoid the two-legged creatures. I mean the two-legged **mammals** (for birds do not do one any harm and are good to eat, when one is clever enough to catch them).

The tabby kitten's contact with the human species had been exceedingly nasty: half-a-dozen evil smelling and yelling boys had cornered the poor young beast at the end of a blind alley where, dead with fright he still had courageously faced them all: claws drawn out, and spitting at them as much as he could. Then, one of them had managed to grip him by the tail and, after whizzing him around several times, had brutally flung him to the floor, head downwards, causing his nose to bang against the stones. The kitten had run away from them, stunned and bleeding, and, for two days, could not eat, on account of his sore, swollen lips and aching body. The episode left him a terror of the two-legged mammal in general, and of the younger ones of the species in particular. He would run for his life at the approach of any human being, especially at any movement of a human hand towards him. And there existed in his little head a sort of loose association between the two-legged enemy and those huge boxes that went about upon wheels, at terrifying speed, with so much noise and such smells: he had often noticed one of the devils step into or out of such " boxes, " and had seen many sitting in them.

However, in spite of that miserable life, he slowly became a half-grown cat-and a beautiful one, whose thinness was partly hidden by a soft and well-kept angora fur (well-kept, not through the use of any brush and comb, of course, but through the ever-repeated and thorough licking of the animal's rough tongue. Whenever the cat was at rest- neither afraid nor too hungry - he would take care of his fluffy coat). And he would have been amazed, had one been able to let him somehow know that he was enduring all his hardships in order to obtain, one day, the supreme joy of meeting once more a two-legged creature who was not a devil; one who had loved him, and whom he had loved, not long before. For not even in his wildest dreams did a meeting memory of her enter his dim consciousness. It was-or seemed-as though she had never crossed his path.

Fortunately for him, the merciless struggle for life- the daily search of some twenty dust-heaps for scraps of skinny meat or, maybe, just one or two bits of dry bread, lost under kitchen ashes; the nightly hunt for mice or crawling creatures, black beetles and such, fit to eat, failing anything better,- did not leave him time to become aware of any "aspirations" or even of desires beyond that of stilling his hunger, of avoiding pain, and of sleeping, whenever too tired to go on hunting for food. He was not quite old enough yet to appreciate the presence of female cats. And had he been, like the two-legged ones, gifted with the power of speech, his definition of " happiness " would have been a negative one. " Not to be hungry; not to be frightened; not to be in pain, **that is** to be happy, " he would have said. For he knew nothing better.

And yet **she** was coming; **she,** the Friend of Creatures, specially the Friend of Felines. She was crossing the sea and she was crossing a continent to hold him once more in her arms,- although she did not know it herself. Among the many forces that drove her on and on was, along with her own will to serve her sacred Cause to the utmost of her capacity... a cat's destiny.

"He was a pretty kitten, with a sweet little round face"

However, in spite of that miserable life, he slowly became a half-grown cat

137

CHAPTER XIII

THE STRENUOUS WAY

She was coming…

The miserable young cat that had once been Long-whiskers, and then, Sandy, was not yet six months old, and she was already sailing across the Mediterranean.

It was night: a warm, moonlit night, through which the eye distinguished very few stars and hardly any horizon. Heliodora was standing on the front-deck, her face to the wind-absorbed in the splendour of her surroundings and in the thrill of feeling herself " on her way, " in the service of the one Cause she had always lived for. It seemed to her as though she was progressing into an infinity of light, over the shining silver sea, into the shining, phosphorescent sky which prolonged it, and was one with it.

"Les deux goufres ne font qu'un abîme sans borne
De tristesse, de paix, et d' éblouissement. … [1]

Again, like on her desperate journey to Europe, nearly twelve years before, she recalled the verses of Leconte de Lisle, one of her favourite poets, and let her spirit merge into the double abyss.

Far, far away, beyond hundreds of miles of water and land, the cat was scratching in the refuse, next to an overturned dustbin; scratching and scratching in search of some scrap, for he had had practically nothing to eat since the day before. He did not know that " she " existed. His only concern was-something to eat !

She was coming.

On the shining sea, she was gliding-still very far away, yet, nearer and nearer every minute.

Before embarking, she had left Miu in the care of the kind old friend who had already taken charge of Black Velvet. (She had seen Black Velvet again, healthy and happy. But she had not been able to stroke him for he would not condescend to come down from the tree, on a branch of which he lay, watching birds).

Until she had got on board the ship, she sometimes had been sad at the thought of all she was leaving, and had wondered when she would come back again. Her heart had ached every time she had recalled the peaceful little house in the woods, the lamp upon the table full of books, the faithful young comrade seated in his usual corner, with Miu purring on his lap. But now that she was on the sea, she thought of the purpose for which she was travelling: to reach India - a free land; freer than Europe, at any rate and have some of her writings printed there. It was all she could do, just now, for her persecuted comrades and for the everlasting National Socialist faith. She would stop some time in Egypt on her way, and visit a few people; then, sail to Beirut, and go to India overland.

Round her, the sea gleamed under the moon, and the luminous sky prolonged the sea. Deep below her feet she could hear the noise the water made as the ship cut its way through it. The next morning, she would be in Alexandria, and a few hours later in Cairo, greeted by people she had long wished to meet. Every moment brought her nearer.

Separated from her by some two thousand miles of desert land, the cat finally managed to dig a chicken's gizzard out of a heap of mixed stale rice and ashes, and started gnawing at it greedily.

*   *   *

Nearly a month later Heliodora was still in Cairo, in a Greek hotel of Soliman Pasha Street, ill in bed, and wondering when she would be able to get up and continue her journey.

This is how it had happened: she had gone to spend a day or two at Tell-el-Amarna, and wandered from sunrise to sunset from the scattered ruins of the City of the Sun, ancient Akhetaton, to the twenty-five rock-tombs in the neighbouring hills, and to the boundary-stones that mark the limits of the consecrated territory, and back again to the ruins. She had pictured herself the Only-One-of-the-Sun, Living in Truth, seated in glory amidst gardens and artificial lakes there where she then stood in burning, barren sand, and telling his disciples of the mystery of matter and power,-of the Sun-Disc and of the energy within the Sun-rays,-which are the same. And she had imagined him, lifting his hands before the altar of the Sun, in the open court that temple of Aton of which nothing remains, and praising Him and His creation in words that foreshadowed the spirit of her own modern faith:

" Thou hast set every man in his place;
Thou hast made them different in shape,
in the colour of their skins and in speech.
As a Divider, Thou hast divided the foreign people
from one another..."[2]

And from the torrid desert, the reverberation of which penetrated her and nearly made her faint, her mind had rushed back to the Leader, whose Sign she boldly wore. Had he not written of the basic tenets of his Teaching:

"Our new ideas, which are entirely in keeping with the original meaning of things. " ?[3]

And at the thought of the everlastingness of his doctrine of Life, of which the very best hymns of the world's hazy past appeared to her as an echo, and which the future would continue proclaiming from age to age, forever, she had felt as though she had been lifted beyond herself with joy.

But she had exhausted herself in her struggle to face the flame of the sky and the burning breath of the sands, and had, again after many years, known the torture of thirst And at sunset, as she had walked back, leaving the purple cliffs behind her, and seen from a distance, under the palms, amidst the first cultivated tracks of land, the first irrigation furrows reflecting the glory of fleeting twilight, she had run, as to a feast and, as soon as she had reached the first liquid ribbon, thrown herself flat upon the ground, thrust her lips forwards and sucked up the muddy water with delight

She had felt ill in the train, on her way back to Cairo, and remained immobilised in bed ever since, with fever and swollen legs. She was now just beginning to get better, and was trying to brush aside all worries and all questions and to " think of nothing, " when she heard a knock at the door. "Come in !" said she.

The person who stepped into the room was an elderly woman

with bright blue eyes and silver-white hair,- a German woman, whom she had met in Egypt.

Heliodora's face brightened. " Do sit down ! I'm so glad you came ! " exclaimed she, with the unmistakable accent of sincerity. " I'm so happy to see you again ! "

She knew that woman was not a fanatical disciple of Adolf Hitler, but she did not mind. Her visitor was, at any rate, not **against** him (anything **but** that !) and she was a German- his compatriot. Heliodora loved all Germans except the downright enemies of National Socialism, whom she regardied as the enemies of Germany and of Life itself.

After inquiring about her health, the visitor put her a : question : " Would you not rather go back to Germany than continue your journey in the state you are ?" The words had an alluring effect upon Heliodora's mind.

In a flash, she recalled her peaceful little house in the woods; the beauty of dawn and sunset; the fragrance of lilacs and of fir-trees; the young National Socialist who used to speak inspiring words to her, at the fireside; the cats that used to come at night and eat the food she would put for them upon the window-sill. All that was still waiting for her. And the of it brought tears into her eyes. But she reflected and said:

" However much I may be longing to go back, I can't. For then, how can I have my books printed ? That can be done only in a free land. "

And she added, as though to strengthen herself in her resolution to continue travelling eastwards : " It is better to be serving Germany than to be **in** Germany. My writings are, as you know, all I can possibly give the Cause just now. "

The visitor remained a while talking of things of everyday life, giving news of her husband and family, of neighbours and friends; and then, she left.

A few days later, Heliodora was again on her way. She knew she was going to try to have her books printed. But what she did not know was that... a cat was calling her from the depth of misery; a cat that she had held in her arms in two at least of his former births, and that had come into the world again and was suffering, precisely so that he might lie in her arms once more, be it only once; and that she had to be in Teheran on the day appointed by Destiny, and at the appointed hour. **Sho was coming**... coming in spite of herself.

*   *   *

She was coming... Seated near the window, in the railway-carriage, and gazing at the plain over which the Sun was rising in glory, she was on her way to Alexandria. She was thinking to herself that all would, in the end, turn to the advantage of the Cause of life- for the sight of the rising Sun always gave her the elation of future triumph.

She spent two days in Alexandria, putting up at a cheap Greek hotel and wandering for hours along the quays of one of the most splendid harbours in the world, watching tie passers-by, deploring the racial characteristics of many of them, imagining the dreadful melting-pot which the city had been, already in Antiquity- and still is- and recalling by contrast, within her heart, her Leader's eternal words : " The State which, at the epoch of race-mixing, devotes itself to the care of its best racial elements is bound one day to become the ruler of the earth."4 She pictured herself future S.S. regiments of a great Aryan Reich, master of the world, marching along those quays to the rhythm of harsh, aggressive music, in front of the last generation of mongrels, as though these did not exist. And she could not repress the joyous feeling: " I shall have, in my humble way, contributed to that- whenever it comes " But a deeper voice within her bade her sternly brush aside that movement of conceit ! " It is not you, silly fool! It is the irresistible Life-force, that Power Whom they call God, Who will bring about that. Bow down and thank its inscrutible wisdom if It cares at all to use you for the edification of those who believe in Adolf Hitler, the Chosen One '"

At last, she sat upon a bench on the jetty and started eating, out of a paper bag, some black olives which she had bought, for she had taken no food all day. She ate a little of her bread with them and gave the remainder of it to a starving dog.

The next day she was lying upon a rug, on the deck, aboard the Greek steamer " Lydia," on her way to Beirut - lying upon a rug on the deck, facing the immensity of the sky, in which a couple of seagulls were flying majestically, like she had done so many times across the Mediterranean, from West to East and East to West, over thirty years before, on board the " Andros " and the " Patris " and many more Greek ships, always " fourth class without food, " free, happy, alone with her great dreams and tremendous ambitions. The dreams had changed-broadened and become more rational; become " Aryandon " instead of " Hellenism, " and the " Greater Reich that has no boundaries ":- Adolf Hitler's faithful ones inspiring the regeneration of all Aryan nations, and Germany, revered as " Holy Land of the West, "-instead of the " Great Idea " (Megale Idea) of all Hellenes, united into one large Greek State stretching all round the Aegian Sea on all sides. And the ambitions had become more and more staggering, and even defeat had not crushed them, but fanned them, on the contrary, into something immense " beyond Germany and beyond our times. " She recalled the books she was planning to have printed. It occurred to her that the words she had written in praise of her Fuhrer and of his doctrine would still be true in millions of years to come-true for ever-even though nobody should know they were hers, even though nobody should know of them **at all.** And that certitude poured unshakable serenity into her heart. She felt as happy, as free and as young as she had in the days she had lain upon a rug on the deck of the " Andros " or of the " Patris ," reading Palamas' " Legend of the One-who-never-wept "[5] or Nietzsche's " Will to power, " when she was seventeen.

But she did not know that a task was awaiting her, already appointed to her by Destiny; a task as unique as, any written creation, if not more so, although it was apparently very simple: that of picking up a dying cat that had, without having, himself, the slightest recollection of it, been born in misery and suffered all his life in order to meet her again.

*   *   *

She was coming…leaning over the railing of the ship, in the port of Beirut she was now enumerating, to a young Syrian who had spent more than a year in Cairo and who seemed intelligent, the different reasons that the Moslem world and the European disciples of Adolf Hitler had to stand together in the struggle against Jewry. She knew, no doubt, that the Arabs' hostility to the Jews had very little in common with that of her German and English comrades and with her own. But she cleverly put stress upon their apparent similarity and, the conversation being carried on in French, she summed up her point of view with a quotation out of Racine's " Andromaque ":

   " Nos ennemis communs devraient nous réunir. "[6]
(she had learnt the whole play by heart, for her own pleasure, at the age of twelve, and still remembered parts of it fairly well).

She was pleased when the young Syrian admitted to her that he looked upon Adolf Hitler as " the greatest of all Europeans "; but that satisfaction could not outweigh her sadness at the sudden thought that so many Aryans refuse to accept even that much.

She remained two days in Beirut, and two days in Damascus where she spent the best of her time in the quiet coolness of the Omayyad Mosque, meditating upon all that a prominent German National Socialist had told her in Egypt about the necessity of using the forces of the non-Aryan world in the double struggle-against Jew-ridden parliamentary Democracy, on one hand, and Communism on the other. She remembered the tragic words: " Now, after the defeat of 1945, we can no longer do it **by ourselves;** we need powerful allies..." Heliodora would have much preferred her comrades to be able to carry on the fight alone. She was wondering why the East, that she had loved, years and years before, now appeared to her so indifferent, so **foreign.** Was it (by contrast) because of her prolonged close contact with **real** Europe, specially with real German National Socialists ? And yet... it would be in the broad-minded East,- freer than post-war Europe a thousand times- that she would, if at all, have her writings printed. How ? With what means ? She did not know. But on she went, untiringly. The heavenly Powers would help her for the sake of the divine Cause.

She was coming....-now rolling through the burning wilderness of Iraq in a bus.

Vague shapes and pale colours- patches of watery light blue that seemed to change places at the limit of the immense expanse of dust and gravel; hazy greyish hills that turned out to be just waves of whirling sand- or dust- that the torrid wind pushed ever and ever further; shimmering outlines that looked, from a distance, like moving clouds and finally turned out to be hills,- appeared and disappeared at the horizon, while Heliodora wondered how the driver could find his way through that endless, flat, barren country, in which she could distinguish no landmarks.

The bus rolled all day and, at nightfall, reached a sort of settlement: warehouses, Customs-offices, and other such official buildings; modern refreshment rooms and, side by side, a few primitive sheds and huts.

It was not the first time Heliodora was following the desert-route between Damascus and Baghdad: she had done so twenty years before, on her return to India from the Middle East (with the only difference that she had then **sailed** back from Basra, through the Persian Gulf). She remembered a halt in the midst of the desert-an old fort upon a hillock; a picturesquely-dressed man of the purest Arab type standing in the arched doorway, like an evocation of another age; a primitive little inn nearby, where a Greek fellow-traveller had treated her to a cup of coffee; and an old gramophone that had been playing Arabic songs... She vividly recalled the beauty of those nostalgic melodies under the first stars; the wilderness all round the tiny group of travellers; and the name of the spot: Rutbaj. Was **this** brand-new seat of trade and of officialdom the **same spot** ? She asked someone : " Is this Rutbaj ?" And as the man said " yes," she felt depressed.

She was coming, however. Whatever changes the East might have undergone within the past ten or twenty years, she was coming. It was, this time, neither the " picturesque East " of her adolescent dreams, nor the East full of memories of Aryan Antiquity-hallowed old "Aryavarta " which could be coaxed into adding " the latest great Aryan ; Incarnation " to its time-honoured heroes and gods-that attracted her now. She knew

146

it would take long years for the "great Aryan Incarnation" of our times to receive world-wide divine honours **in spite of defeat in war.** No; all she now sought was the East of freedom and of toleration- of freedom, because of apathy; of toleration, because of indifference,- the East in which one could print whatever one liked, provided one paid. She knew she never again would have a home: nor the one in which she had spent her early youth; nor the one in Calcutta, with more cats purring around her; nor the one in the heart of Germany, the little house in the woods that she had loved so much and yet forsaken. And she did not really care. Her brothers in faith were her only family, the future Great Reich, of which she longed to become an honorary citizen, her only home, and the echo (if any) of a few sentences of hers in her comrades' minds, her only immortality.

She did not know that one of the creatures she had loved the most in Calcutta, in the great days of victory and of staggering hopes, had been reborn for her sake, and was now bleeding upon a dust-heap in Teheran, after a nasty child had flung him a stone- bleeding, and waiting for her (he too, without knowing it).

The bus was starting again. She felt the vibrations of the machinery under her seat, then saw the surrounding lights and shadows and lines change places as she went by. Within two minutes she was again rolling through the night towards Baghdad, breathing the breath of the desert.

She was coming.

*   *   *

She watched the Sun rise in majesty over the flat, dry, grey landscape-the same Sun that she used to greet with her arm outstretched, in the cool morning, before her little house in Germany, as His rays reached her through the high trees.

She gazed at Him and whispered, in the language of her Leader, which had become a sacred language to her:

"Heil Dir, Lichtrater allwallende !" And she added in Sanskrit, as though wishing to re-link all that her Aryan faith meant to her with a whole world of thought and fervour that had also been partly hers : "**Aum Suryam ! Namah, namah !**"

After stopping for a short time at a last inhabited spot, the bus at last reached Baghdad, at about ten o'clock in the moaning.

Heliodois would have liked to spend a few days in the old city of the Abbasside Caliphs- to seek and meet once more the kind Hindu friends whose hospitality she had enjoyed on her first trip; to revisit the ruins of Babylon, so nearby. She had ample time, apparently. Her books had waited so long for the printing-press, that they could afford to wait another week. But **something** was urging her not to stop; causing her to feel as though she had been in a hurry. What was it ? The fact that she had very little money ? However little she had, she **could have** managed to remain at least a day or two. The fact that there were no organised excursions to Babylon in July, and that she really could not afford to take a taxi all to herself, there and back ? But she could have wandered about Baghdad without revisiting Babylon. It was not that which drove her on. It was something of which she did not know: a poor, half-grown tabby cat- that could have been beautiful, had it not been so miserable- limping from one dustbin to another in search of scraps of decaying food, a thousand miles away from her; a cat whose Destiny was to bring him to see her, or feel her, once more, after twelve years of separation and whose deeper, unconscious self was calling her : " Come ! Come ! Don't waste a minute lest you should not reach me in time. I have lived a life of misery so that I might die in your arms. Come !"

She was coming... She left Baghdad the very same day, a little before sunset, in a small, overcrowded bus, in which she had been given a seat near the window, on the last wooden bench but one, at the back. She had been waiting the whole afternoon in a primitive, overcrowded " place ", in one of the poorest, noisiest (and dirtiest) localities of the rapidly expanding city, to get that uncomfortable seat

*   *   *

She was coming... The bus was rushing through the golden

148

evening, full-speed, along the road to Kermancha. The road was dusty, and extremely uneven. At every depression, the bus would suddenly sink, and come up again with a powerful jerk, which meant that Heliodora was bluntly projected four or five inches above her seat, only to fall back immediately upon the hard wood, getting bruised every time, yet thanking her stars that she had not being flung straight out of the window, which had neither a glass pane nor any bars for protection.

At first, she tried to grin and bear it without complaining. Nobody complained. Was not she, a National Socialist, to prove herself at least as tough as any of her co-travellers, none of whom had (apart from one or two Iranis, with exceptionally classical features) the slightest physical relationship with Aryandom ? She made it a point of honour to remain silent and even recalled in her mind the famous motto of the Stoics : "Put up with (suffering) and abstain from (complaining.) [1] It seemed to her as though the old Greek words, faint echo of a world that she had once, long, long before, so enthusiastically accepted as hers, gave her strength. She also thought of her German comrades who had suffered and died for the glorious Faith- theirs **and** hers,- and for the Reich of her dreams, without a word. And she felt small. The very thought of **them** in that darkening wilderness, amidst that rough crowd, so far away from Europe, worked upon her as a spell of pride. She forced herself to concentrate her mind upon the difference that existed between the ethics of the Stoics and those of her own faith, in spite of the stress laid by both upon will-power and indifference to personal sufferings. And she continued to be tossed up and down as the bus rolled on towards the east, towards Iran.

However, as a particularly violent jerk nearly threw her out of the window, she cried out aloud while struggling in vain to catch hold of the wooden frame, too far ahead of her seat. The whole bus burst out laughing. Aching, humiliated, enraged, Heliodora shouted back in Turkish (for she did not know how to say it in Arabic or Persian): " Zemdeme !" " You go to hell !" Her fellow-travellers laughed all the more. And she hated them for laughing; and felt doubly miserable, doubly ashamed for having lost her temper in front of them.

The bus halted for a few minutes in the night. Heliodora saw a few tents pitched on each side of the track, and one or two huts. Men-some dressed in the picturesque loose robes of the desert-folk, others in tattered international shirts and pants,-were sitting or standing about. There were a number of young boys among them. There were donkeys, also little grey donkeys that stood still, staring blankly before them, listless, worn-out, utterly miserable; quite a number of dogs, all of them skin and bone. Heliodora got down from the bus and started giving the animals the bread she had bought in Baghdad for her journey. A skeleton-like bitch, with hanging paps, heavy with milk, was just thrusting herself forward to seize a chunk of bread that the woman had thrown to her, when she suddenly ran, howling, into the wilderness: one of the boys had flung a sharp stone at her and hit her right upon her belly. The same boy then stood grinning before Heliodora, begging for " bakshish ". But she turned away from him in indignation: " Bakshish ? Not for you, dirty coward ! " she cried, even though she thought no one could understand her (she would have beaten him, scratched him, trampled him, till he, too, would have howled with pain, had she not known beforehand that the whole crowd would have taken his defence, and that it is useless to try to fight with bare fists, alone against fifty or more).

She was going back to the bus when a dark, frizzy haired young man in well-cut European clothes addressed her in English:

" You are angry because the child hit that poor bitch ?" he said.

" Of course I am. He hit her so hard that one can still hear her howling. But if he thinks he will get any money from me he makes a mistake. Money, indeed ! A beating, a beating till he is more than half dead-that is all the slimy coward deserves "

" You see," pursued the would-be humanitarian, who had learnt oil technology and democratic principles somewhere in the U.S.A., " you must try to understand these people: they are poor, very poor; and they don't like dogs. Nobody likes dogs here. They are a nuisance."

"And **I**," replied Heliodora, shivering with passion; " I hate people who have no regard for living creatures. I look upon

150

them as a nuisance, and hold that they should be destroyed "

The well-dressed defender of human priority walked away. From the hostile glances of her fellow-travellers, Heliodora gathered that he had translated to them what she had said. Only an old, very old and kind-looking desert-dweller, seated at the entrance of a tent on the roadside, shook his head and muttered something which, from the expression of his face, seemed to suggest, if not wholehearted approval, at least understanding. She looked back and faintly smiled at him. She imagined him to be a devout Moslem and, for a minute, recalled the Prophet of Islam- a man who hated cruelty, as all true warriors do, and who, although he had a very definite predilection for **cats**, and looked upon dogs as " unclean " and had forbidden his followers to " touch " them, had certainly never urged anybody to **hit** or hurt any creature.

She wrapped up her remaining bread for " another time "-when she could give it to some dog without any jealous child noticing her- and went and took back her seat in the bus, more alone than ever. The howling of the wounded bitch had ceased under the stars. The bus rolled on, full-speed. At every jerk, Heliodora felt as though she would faint and fall. But she did not.

The border between Iraq and Iran was crossed. Late in the night, the bus reached Kermancha and halted at the entrance of a broad, open courtyard with an arched gallery along one side of it.

*   *   *

All the passengers got down. Heliodora, if only for the sake of relaxation, went and took a stroll and had a look at the surroundings. At first, she had intended to remain a couple of days in Kermancha: she knew the famous rock-reliefs and inscriptions of Behistun are not far from there, and she had always longed to see them. It would have been easy: she would only have had to go and tell the man seated at what could have been called the " office "-a little room containing a table and a bench, not far from the bus-stop - to reserve a seat for her in one of the northbound buses that were to pass, perhaps the next day, perhaps the day after. **Somebody** in the office would understand English- or Greek, or Turkish, or Hindustani, or perhaps German, or some other language she could speak, (there always are polyglotts to be found in the East). And there would be some corner where she would be able to keep her luggage, and some other corner in which she would be able to spend the night- or perhaps there would be a guest-house near the rocks of Behistun ? It did not make the slightest difference whether she reached India in three weeks' time, or in three weeks and three days.

And yet... some intuition, or some telepathic call, at any rate something stranger than any logical thinking, was holding her back and urging her, as insistently as ever, along the road to Teheran. It was the miserable, hungry, wounded cat, beautiful in spite of all in his long, stripy fur,- Sandy; Long-whiskers, reborn in suffering only to feel the touch of her hands once more- that was calling her over miles and hundreds of miles of wilderness, from the other end of Iran : " Come ! Come for my sake ! The rocks of Behistun can wait; I can't. "

She thought, without realising why : "Let it be on another occasion ! The reliefs and inscriptions are not going to run away, and I shall revisit Iran, although I don't know **when**." And, just as she had in Baghdad, she decided to continue her journey without a break.

But she did not like the crowded caravanserail- and especially not the loud-speaker, transmitting radio music to the many travellers. Most of the latter had started eating chicken pilaw that was being served to them from a nearby kitchen, or food that they had brought with them. Some were preparing their meal upon open fires, in the courtyard. The women and children were seated, most of them, with their brightly coloured metal suit-cases and enormous bundles, in a huge hall that opened into the arched gallery. Their quarters were the noisiest of all, and Heliodora shuddered at the prospect of spending the night there. It would be at least an hour or two before everybody had finished eating and gone to sleep- and she was longing to rest. In addition to that she pictured herself babies crying, and the anxious mothers constantly switched on the light to see what the matter was, and she remaining awake all night. (She had always resented the presence of so many babies in the buses, trains and waiting-rooms of the East). So she inquired whether she could not spend the night m the empty bus. There was no objection, save that one imagined that she would not be comfortable.

" I shall sleep far better there alone than in the dormitory, " said she.

" But there is a place reserved for women and children ..."

" I know," replied she, somewhat embarrassed, for she knew it was useless to express the reasons of her reluctance: nobody would understand them. "I know; still, I'd rather be in the bus, alone."

She was locked in-for safety. She then spread a few newspapers upon the floor, between the two rows of seats, and lay upon them, wrapped in her coat, using her handbag as a pillow. And she slept... after the accursed loudspeaker had at last become silent.

Far away, in Teheran, the tabby cat was walking along Roosevelt Avenue, crying in the warm starry night " Mee-u ! Meee-u !" like he had fifteen years before, when " she " had heard him, a poor black-and-white kitten, and his distressed mother, and come down to fetch them both. It was not hunger, this time, that caused him to cry: he had gulped down a whole heap of chicken's entrails that he had found in a dust-bin, and then caught and ate a mouse for his " dessert ". It was not lust either: he was barely six months old. It was some mysterious uneasiness that possessed him, and that even a two-legged one could not have defined- let alone a cat; some unexplainable fear, and, at the same time, some extraordinary, joyous prescience.

O Cat whose purr had once sufficed to tell her what she needed to know in order to remain herself; Cat, who, without being able to grasp human affairs, had yet saved her from the spirit of questioning that leads to heresy, you now dimly felt that **she was coming**, that she was **on her way,** that the time of supreme trial and of supreme fulfilment, which you had accepted before that miserable present birth, was drawing nigh. And your mew was a mew of terror-a call for help-like then, in the dark Calcutta " go-down ", and a mew of welcome to the " Two-legged goddess. "

*　　　*　　　*

She woke up at day-break, after a short, but sound, dreamless sleep. She gathered her newspapers and folded them up neatly, in order to use them again for the second night in case she did not manage to find clean ones; for she was not to reach Teheran till the evening of the following day- the third day after her departure from Baghdad. She got down as soon as the bus was unlocked, washed her face, arms and legs the best she could, at a tap in the crowded courtyard, drank a glass of tea- which was sweet, and too strong, and which she did not like - only because she had been told that there was no coffee, and got back and seated herself in her place in the bus. The other passengers came in after they had finished their breakfast, and the journey continued.

The road was not quite as bad as the day before. And it was morning. There is joy in every landscape, however barren, for some time after sunrise. Heliodora let her eyes rest upon the reddish-brown road, upon the reddish-brown empty expanses on either side of it, and soon, upon the succession of harmoniously shaped hill-ranges that appeared at the horizon. She was impressed by the beauty and variety of their colouring: ochre, greyish-yellow, greyish or reddish-brown, in the foreground; pinkish-grey, bluish-grey, and pale violet, as their distance increased. And as one drove nearer, their colours would change, and new hazy blues and purples would appear behind those that had merged into warmer foreground shades. She was also impressed by the scarcity of people one met along the road, and by the beauty of some of those ones did meet, now and then, at long, long intervals. She automatically interpreted the contrast between the features of those rare passers - by and those of most of her co-travellers who, even when Iranis, were town-people. " Races are purer in the countryside, in whatever land it be, " thought she, as the bus rolled on.

There were two breaks during the journey, before the long halt on the second night. Wherever the bus stopped, there were always a few trees, sometimes many; and the travellers could sit at a table in some quaint and cool little inn, in the common hall of which there generally was water spouting up from the middle of a fairly large, square or rectangular pool, made of stone or marble (or " imitation "). Customers would sit all round it and eat and drink to the crystalline music of the water-drops. But everywhere Heliodora noticed skeleton-like dogs and famishing cats, afraid to come near a human being, and their sight made her feel indignant, and hardened her heart against man and whomsoever proclaims the " rights of all men." In her eyes, men who have no love for other living creatures have also no rights. She bought bread and curds for the animals, and saw to it that no two-legged mammal snatched away the food before they dared come and eat it. She gave a few coppers to the beggars in order not to look too partial and thus rouse hostility against herself.

After half an hour spent in a cool, shady spot, the burning barren land through which she was travelling seemed hotter and dustier than ever. Heliodora, however, was absorbed in her thoughts. She was trying to picture herself what Iran had looked like in the days in which Aryans, brothers of those of Vedic India, had ruled Iran, centuries later, in the time of the Achemenide Kings, and then, under the successors of Alexander; under the Arsacides and, latest of all, under the Sassanides. The Arab conquest (651 A.D.) and the spreading of Islam had been to Iran what Roman conquest and subsequent christianisation had been to Europe. Heliodora, who willingly described herself as a " nationalist of every land ", would have welcomed a "back to Aryan Iran" movement, parallel to the great European upheaval of which she herself was such a supporter. But could such a movement ever take place? " Perhaps," thought she, "if we rise again one day in Europe, and if some of these people still have enough Aryan blood and Aryan virtues to take the lead of the others."

She decided to try to find out-indirectly-how far some of the most " Indo-European " looking among her fellow-travellers could be brought to share her views, if ever they had proper leaders. The woman in front of her had exceptionally fine Aryan features. She was travelling with six children, the eldest of whom might have been ten years old. She did not speak anything else but Persian. But her husband, who had worked in the Oil Company at Abadan, spoke English. When night came and when the travellers got down, Heliodora drew his notice by offering some sweets to the children and asking him what the latter were called- she believed in the magic of names and in the deeper instinct that urges a parent to chose them, whenever rigid custom does not rule out free choice.

" My eldest child, a daughter, is called Farida, " said he; " but the two others have Iranian names: Parivash, and Mahivaah." " And your sons ?" she asked.

" The eldest,-my second child - is called Mohammed Abbas. But I also gave Iranian names - Cyrus and Ardeshir - to the younger ones. "

Heliodoia's face brightened. " You are beginning to wake up to true nationalism, " said she, with a smile. And she added : " We too, in Europe, had startedling our children names in harmony with our blood and soil. Germany, the natural leader of European nations, had stressed that point and set the example. But, of course, since the disaster of 1945. "

The man asked her whether she was German. She spoke the truth, and said : " No, I am not "

"Then, why do you believe Germany to be " the natural leader of European nations ?" asked the Persian.

"Because she gave birth to Adolf Hitler, who laid down for us the principles of eternal wisdom that we had forgotten for centuries, " was Heliodora's answer.

People gathered around her as they heard the Name that has echoed throughout the world. The man, who had been working in Abadan translated whatever she said. It was, for her, a joy to praise her Führer before that strange audience, in the heart of Iran. It reminded her of the years she had spent in India preaching the fundamental identity of the National Socialist principles and of those on which Hindu civilisation has been conceived, and the caste hierarchy established; also the identity of National Socialist ethics and of those implied in the Teaching of detached violence, written in the Bhagawad Gita. How she had been happy during those years of apparent increasing influence, when she had, in her easy enthusiasm,

156

imagined herself preparing the way for her Leader's New World Order ! Now, of course, it was " Aryan Iran " of which she spoke; of Iran, from King Cyrus to King Jizdedjerd, with its cult of Light, still alive among the Parsis of India (and even in Persia itself) ; with its invincible language, the roots of which are the same as those of Sanskrit and of all the Aryan tongues of the earth. And remembering that, in spite of all, most Persians are Mohammadans since the 7th Century A.D., she cleverly spoke also of the Islamic world of today in its length and breadth and with its many races and sub-races, as of the natural ally of all Aryans who are conscious of the Jewish danger.

" Our Adolf Hitler, " said she at last, "came to show all nations-first his own, and then other Aryan nations, but also **the non-Aryan ones;** all **real** nations of the world the way of true nationalism, i.e., the way of true collective pride and collective virtue, which is the Way of Blood and Soil; the way leading to God, in fact, since man's blood and the soil of his ancestors are the only things which he can neither acquire nor alter according to his will; that he cannot reject, even if he denies them, even if he becomes unworthy of them-God-given treasures. That is why I say : " He spoke God's own words, like all true prophets do. That is why I say : "He is a prophet, not a mere politician. " (In India, she would not have said " a prophet " but " an Incarnation of the Divine. " Here, she felt her **language** had to be different, whatever were her personal views).

The dark young man who had expressed such a dislike of dogs the night before, now put in a word:

" Why did he persecute the Jews if he was, as you say, one sent by God ?" said he, referring to Adolf Hitler. " And what do you Nazis all mean with your ' Jewish danger ?" Aren't Jews human beings like any others."

" Human beings are, when dangerous, precisely **more** dangerous than any other living creatures, " replied Heliodora. " And these people art dangerous **as a whole, as a people,** precisely because they try to teach the rest of mankind, and specially the most gifted and healthiest races, to deny or mock the eternal Doctrine of Blood and Soil, while **they** (although they are anything but pure-blooded) proclaim it for themselves with religious fanaticism, even when they maintain that they have done away with every religion. "

" That's all nonsense ! " exclaimed the young man. "All Jews are not Zionists. Many believe as I do that there are no races, only human beings, but rich ones and poor ones, exploiters and exploited; and only want that exploitation of man by man to come to an end, and all men to enjoy the riches of the earth to the full."

On hearing these words Heliodora understood that the young man was a Jewish Communist. He did not speak to her again, deeming it useless. But several of the other listeners put questions to her, or made remarks. A young Arab, who had learnt English in Egypt, told her that he sincerely admired her Führer. So did a young Irani student who added : " We are a handful in this country who do stand for Aryan regeneration, and honour him as the greatest of all Aryans since Cyrus and Darius the Truthful, the best of our kings. "

Heliodora pictured herself the Doctrine and the cult of her beloved Leader- and, through it, the cult, or at least the reverence of Germany- conquering the whole world according to her life-long dream, in spite of defeat, in spite of stubborn calumny, in spite of widespread indifference; conquering it slowly and irresistibly, as corn grows, or as fruits ripen. And she recalled the words of a German comrade, addressed to her four years before : " Does one **see** corn grow ? or hear it ? So is our onward march: unseen and silent. " Could this indeed be true? thought she.

That night,- her last night on the way to Teheran- she took a long time to fall asleep upon her bed of newspapers, in the bus. Not that the hard, wooden floor felt harder than on the night before: she did not feel it. But she was the prey of a strange excitement, as though she were about to **do** something of great importance; she could not make out **what.** Yet she did know that anything she would do, in earnest and with all her heart, would, ultimately, directly or indirectly, serve the National Socialist Cause, for this was, in her eyes, the very Cause of Life itself. And she was happy, for she entirely identified herself with it and thus, in a way, shared its eternity.

158

From Teheran, like on the night before, came the Cat's feeble mew, calling her desperately;- and calling Fate; the mew that nobody could hear, not even she, but that had drawn her all these weeks, all these months, as implacably as her tremendous dreams, over land and sea and torrid wilderness; over Europe, Greece and Egypt, and along the highways of Syria, Iraq and Iran.

This was her last night. **She was coming**...

* * *

The next day - 9th of July-was the best day of the journey. Heliodora knew she would not have to spend another night on the way. Some of the passengers had also become friendlier since they had heard her speak on the evening before. Nobody made any remarks when, at the halting places, she bought bread for the stray dogs, or curds,- which she then poured out upon some scrap of paper and quietly placed under a bench or in some corner - for the cats. Little Mahivash, who had been observing her for a long time, even felt prompted to do the same, and was overjoyed when her father gave her a spoonful of curds upon an old piece of tin, which she carefully went and laid upon the ground before an emaciated cat. The cat ran away at the child's approach, and a dog- a hungry creature, at any rate, - licked up the curds. Heliodora was touched at the little girl's gesture, and was more seriously than ever prepared to believe in the possibility of "Aryan regeneration in Asia," for in her eyes children's love of living creatures was a sign of noble blood.

She also enjoyed more than ever the crystalline coolness of spouting water in the inns, and the palm-tree thickets nearby, after the long, burning desert-tracks. Even the tea, although much too strong for her taste, and sweet, was beginning to seem tolerable to her.

The bus rolled into Teheran in the late afternoon. Heliodora took leave of the sympathetic family from Abadan as well as from the two young men who had expressed admiration for her Leader on the evening before. She then went and took a room at a hotel owned by Greeks and " not too expensive

"-the " Cyprus Hotel "-which someone had recommended to her.

At last, **she had come.**

1. The two abysses are but one fathomless depth of sadness, of peace and of radiant light.
2. Akhnaton's " Longer Hymn to the Sun."
3. " . unsere neue Auffasung, die ganz dem Ursinn der Dinge entspricht..." (" Mein Kampf," edit. 1939. p. 440).
4. "Ein Staat, der im Zeitalter der Rassenvergiftung sich der Pflege seiler besten rassischen Elemente widmet, muss eines Tages zum Herrn der Erde werden." (" Mein Kampf," edit. 1936, p. 782).
5. "To Parrmythi tou Adakrytou," out of that modern Greek poet's a " Dodekalogos tou gyftou" (" The twelve discourses of the Gypsy "). edit. 1902.
6. "Our common enemies should bring us together." ("Adromaque," Act 1. Scene IV).
7. Anekhou kai apekhou.

CHAPTER XIV

10th OF JULY, 1957

The fated hour had come for the unfortunate tabby tomcat. He was, now, about to suffer what his latest forgotten self-dying Sandy - had chosen in a minute of supreme yearning, a few months before. And this is how he met his destiny:

Some dogs - or perhaps some nasty children, who are even worse, - had started chasing him along Roosevelt Avenue, half way between Takke Avenue and the next great crossing. And he was running like a mad cat, without knowing where he was going; running, with one overwhelming purpose: to escape the monsters; not to hear them an in close pursuit. In fact, he **had** escaped them, and could have gone his way quite peacefully. But he had not escaped the consciousness of their presence; the **fear** of them. It was that fear that maddened him.

As he reached great crossing, he could have turned to the right and run the footpath. But no : there were half-a-dozen shouting street urchins at the corner. They stamped their feet, made violent gestures with their arms, and called out louder than ever as soon as they caught sight of him, so that, completely panic-stricken, the poor cat flung himself across the busy avenue before a car. The car ran over him, dislocating his hind legs, crushing his belly and forcing out of it an inch or two of soiled entrails. He gave a high-pitched shriek and rolled over, shuddering convulsively. The wretched urchins kicked him onto the footpath, where he continued to shudder, while they looked on, laughing and giggling at his plight.

" I am ready to suffer-to suffer anything-provided I may lie in her arms for five minutes," had said dying Sandy, in the silent language of supreme desire, at the crucial moment that decides of rebirth. Now, was it not enough-those six months of misery, and this horrid agony upon the baking-hot asphalt, amidst the jeers of these young sub-men and the total indifference of that crowd of passers-by, every one of whom went his way without even giving the Poor beast a glance ? Had not the one that had been Sandy-and before that, Long-whiskers - yet deserved the ultimate reward of so long and ardent a yearning ? The happiness that such a ransom of suffering was to buy ?

He kept on moving his head and front paws convulsively, while his intestines draggled in the dust, and blood and filth clotted his royal fur. His eyes, wide open, had a glassy stare, as though they were already dead, or nearly so.

Then, at last, the wonder took place: **" she " was there;** she had come; she was at his side, although he could not see her.

*   *   *

She was wearing a cream-coloured dress with a large, ornamented border round the bottom, round the sleeves, and on each side of the opening on the breast-Greek style, - which she had bought in Athens, on this very journey of hers. She had bought it because she liked hand-woven material, hand embroidery and local cut, but also and perhaps more so because of the **" odal "** runes which she had at once noticed among the " ornaments " on the pink, olive-green, light and dark-brown border. **She** had wondered whether the Greek embroideresses had known what they were doing when they had made those odal runes part and parcel of their intricate design. Probably not. But she knew their meaning. And apart from that, they reminded her of J. von Leers' famous book " Odal, or the history of German peasantry " - one of the best books she had ever read. To her, they expressed the survival of Aryan Tradition in Greece to-day, and were a visible link between **real** Greece and eternal Germany, nay, the whole hallowed North. And she wore that dress with pride, as a vestment suited to her Aryan faith. On that day, she was also wearing her gold ear-rings in the shape of swastikas. In Teheran, thought she - in spite of the existence of a " Roosevelt Avenue " (and of a " Churchill Avenue " and of a " Stalin Avenue " also) in commemoration of the sinister meeting of 1943 - nobody would care. And it was such a joy to her to wear them: a gleaming profession of faith. Why not ? Other women wore gold crosses, or Jewish stars. Why should she not wear her Sign ? She wore it with the

162

usual elation of defiance.

Thus attired, she was crossing the Avenue when that convulsive lump of fur and that circle of noisy urchins, on the opposite footpath, attracted her attention. Scenting some new horror-she had seen so many !-she ran, and was on the spot within a minute. At first, she imagined the boys had half-killed the cat, and her flaming eyes looked daggers at them. Then she saw the dragging knot of entrails, the motionless, dislocated hind legs... " More likely he has been run over, " she thought, picking up the poor creature as softly as she could; supporting his bleeding intestines with her hand. The children watched her and laughed. She cursed them : " You filthy, heartless brats, " cried she (and she was so beyond herself with indignation that it did not come to her mind that the urchins could not understand her speech) ; " you young cowards ! I wish you all perish in the same manner, under the wheels of the first invader's tanks - and I could not care less who the invader be, as long as you suffer, you devils !'"

A few people gathered round her and forced the bewildered boys to disperse. A man asked Heliodora in English what she was expecting to do with this dying cat.

" Give him some chloroform, of course, or some ether; anything that will grant him a painless death. What else is there to be done, in the state he is in ? "

" They will not give you any " replied the man. You can try and ask, if you like. There is a chemist's shop just here, and another round the corner. But I doubt it." " But why ? Why ?" cried Heliodora. " I shall pay for it; pay any price they ask. "

" They won't give you any for a cat," replied the man. " And if you say it is for a human patient, they'll want a doctor's prescription. I know these people. But you can always try "

She tried, and found out that the man was right. With the cat in her arms, she went to three chemist's shops along the avenue, only to get the same answer every time;

" We don't sell ether or chloroform for cats and dogs " She felt disgusted and hated mankind. " Lord of Life and Death, Whoever Thou art, " played she within her heart, for the millionth time, " treat them, individually and collectively, always and everywhere, as they treat dumb creatures.

And remember me, when it shall please Thee to strike them. Make me an instrument of Thy divine vengeance !"

In a flash, she pictured herself at the head of a concentration camp in the new world of her dreams - a concentration camp full of such two-legged mammals as these, who believe that " man " is everything, and other creatures nothing. (Such ones would surely be Anti-Nazis : all supporters of the " rights " of man, the " dignity " of man, the "endless possibilities " of man, etc..., generally are). How she would gladly " take it out of them ! " - prove to them how thoroughly she believed man is nothing and how little she loved him, with the exception, of course, of a minority of real aristocrats of blood and character; supermen in the making.

She slowly walked back in the direction of Roosevelt Avenue and turned to her left as she came to the crossing. Blood and filth stained her hands and her dress. But she thought only of the cat. How long would his agony last ?

*   *   *

She held him against her breast with infinite care and infinite love. And she stroked his glossy head, and kissed it, as only she could kiss a cat.

At first, when she had picked him up and taken him in her arms, the poor beast had experienced a feeling of immense relief. He had lived in hell, all his life, and known, from the beginning, all round him, nothing but cruelty or criminal indifference, nearly as bad. Along with torturing hunger, hardly ever completely stilled, fear had been his main experience - fear of kicks; fear of sharp stones flung at him; fear of boiling water (or be it even cold water) ; fear of other creatures such as dogs; above all, fear of the two-legged creature, the devil among devils; fear, hunger and pain; pain, hunger and fear. He had seldom ever purred since he had last sucked his mother and slowly gone to sleep in the warmth of her coat, the night before she had met her death. And then, all of a sudden, he had known a more maddening fear than ever, and fallen into a more appalling hell :- a hell of excruciating pain; of pain that shattered his nerves and made his head whirl. And just as one confusedly continues to hear, beyond the more exacting sounds of one's immediate surroundings, the persistent noise of the street, so did he retain, beyond the torment of agony, the dim awareness of universal cruelty.

But what was that unconceivable power that came down to him and lifted him, as softly and as lovingly as his mother used to, long, long before ?- and that turned away the devils that were making fun of his pain ? What was that unknown, soothing radiance that penetrated him, and forced the pain in his back, the pain in his squashed belly, the pain in his whirling head to recede, at least for a second ? What was that touch ?- that arm that supported him ? That lap, in which he now lay, as he once had against his mother's fur, in the only happy days he could have remembered, had he been able to remember anything, in his agony ? (for Heliodora had stooped down, in order to let him rest more at ease). What was that hand that caressed him - him, who had never been caressed ? Was it the Great Feline Mother, Queen of love, shoreless and fathomless Night, mother of all Life, into which all life is absorbed a all suffering ends - immense projection of his own mother, long dead - who had come to take him away from this world of fear and pain ?

But the cool, sweet Presence had a human face - not like that of most two-legged devils, of course, but yet, a face of the same shape as theirs, only loving, earnest, fervent, instead of gleefully cruel or coarsely indifferent: the contrary of theirs. As through a haze, he could now see her two large dark eyes, from which a tear dropped into his fur. And her mouth touched his poor head, still so beautiful - uncrushed.

" My poor stripy puss, " she murmured; " it is for you, for you alone that I came over those hundreds of miles of desert-land ! I know it now. "

He was resting in her lap. The convulsions of his body gradually ceased. Then, from the depth of an unfailing, mysterious cat-memory, that more intellectual creatures can neither grasp nor imagine, an unearthly flash of knowledge came to the dying beast : " She - it is she; the Two-legged goddess ! " And through his silky coat stained with blood, Heliodora felt the vibration of a supreme purr. And that purr meant : " I have been waiting for you twelve years. And I have suffered all this so that I might die in your arms, as I so longed to ! ”

EPILOGUE.
FACE TO THE STARS.

In the middle of the night, somewhere along the desert-track between Mashed and Zahedan, the bus had halted: it needed repair; and it would take quite an hour or two before it could start again. The passengers were requested to get down and wait. They were told that, less than two hundred yards away, there was a cluster of huts, where water was available.

Many started walking in that direction, because they were thirsty; most of the others followed, because they had nothing to do and thought a little exercise would do them no harm, after their long immobility upon the hard seats. One or two men and women, with little children, who had brought food and drink with them, remained near the bus, opened their parcels, and began eating, seated in a circle.

After wandering about for a while, and getting accustomed to the darkness, Heliodora went and chose herself a place sufficiently near the bus for her to be able to hear when it would start, and sufficiently far away for her to be alone. And she lay upon her back in the warm sand, face to the starry sky.

It was a moonless night. And the landscape was rugged. Dark mountain ranges could be seen **at the horizon, in all** directions but one, and the peculiar light of the sky, that did not shine **upon** them, made them appear darker and more compact than ever. And one could not distinguish any shades in them. The land was also covered with darkness; one could hardly differentiate sand from rock, save through touch. And although the distance that separated her from them was short, and the land in between, flat, Heliodora could not see the huts from the place where she was lying. But, above black hills and dark earth, the night sky hung and shone in all its glory, each side of the Milky Way. And the dedicated woman let her soul merge into that luminous Infinity, while her body relaxed in the warm sand, like a tired child in its bed. She worshipped the splendour of the Cosmos, aspiring to put herself in tune with it. And in it and through it, she sought the Unattainable One: the Soul of the Dance of the milliards of nebulae, that no finite being can conceive.

*   *   *

She was on her way from Mashed, the sacred city of Iran, to Zahedan, on the border of Balushistan, where she was to take the train to Quetta, from where she would reach Lahore, Delhi, Calcutta.

Would she, at last, manage to have her books printed ? She needed money, in order to do so, but had none. Would she find work, in India ? An Indian official in Egypt had told her it was " practically impossible. " How would she live, then, and what would she do ? In fact, although the country was familiar to her, she did not know where she was going.

But the majesty of the starry sky pervaded her, and she did not care. She forgot the bus, and the passengers, and the journey, and space and time - as though she were to remain forever upon that bed of sand, under the divine light of the galaxies. The thought of the cat that had died in her arms in Teheran, over a fortnight before, crossed her mind. " And even if I never can have my writings printed, it does not matter, " felt she. " That cat, at least, has not died unloved and alone. To comfort him was worth the long strenuous journey. Pasupati, Lord of Creatures, I bless Thee for having guided me in time to the spot; and I adore Thee ! " She knew-and the sight of the sky full of stars only helped her to become once more aware of the elation this knowledge gave her - that the same eternal Life that had purred to her in the dying beast, flourished invincibly in countless far-away worlds as on this earth; that death was but a passage to new life; and that, at the root of life, there was Light: Light that had always sprung, always shone, from distance to distance, out of the abysmal womb of shoreless Night, like this dust of stars in the dark sky.

And she recalled the earthly Faith for which she lived...In that Radiant sky, there were stars millions and milliards of light-years away from our little planet, and away from one another;

stars of which the rays, that she now perceived, had started their journey through space at the time this earth was a swamp out of which emerged forests of gigantic ferns, under torrential downpours of warm water, or even long, long before, when it was but a whirling mass of lava - a world in the making. What was this earth - and what was Germany, and all the pride of militant National Socialism, - to that staggering, impersonal Infinity ? Less than a speck of dust ! And yet...wherever divine Light had given birth to Life within those endless expanses; wherever there were living races of thinking or unthinking creatures upon any planet, born of any Sun, the principles at the basis of the struggle for survival, the divine laws of racial selection proclaimed by the greatest of all Germans, Adolf Hitler, held good, as they did here; as they always had done, in the history of our tiny Earth. And the implacable ethics that express those eternal Laws of life, were the divine ethics of fathomless space, for ever and ever. Glory to Him who proclaimed them - be He, in his latest manifestation as in all others, but a flash in Time without end !-and to those of his disciples, they too, creatures of a second, who lived and died, faithful to his spirit ! For He is the One - who comes-back : the Soul of the starry Dance that takes on, again and again, the garb of mortal frailty, to teach finite beings the Rule of all the worlds.

And Heliodora felt even happier and more certain of victory than she would have at the sight of the most gorgeous display of her comrades' conquering power. " Our definitive defeat would mean the defeat and end of Life itself, **here**, " thought she, " it is clearly said so in 'Mein Kampf ' ¹ " But **even then** our struggle carried on by other beings, would continue, wherever Life exists." And she felt invincible, along with all her persecuted comrades. Once more she had integrated the Hitler faith and the cult of Aryan aristocracy into the worship of the starry Sky, Light and Life eternal.

" Lord who art the Essence of this radiant immensity, " she prayed, " it is Thee, Thee alone that I have always worshipped, be it in the loveliness of dumb creatures, be it in the pride, intelligence and conquering will-power of my Leader and of those who are nearer to him than I. For Thou shinest in them;

Thou art they. Guide me wherever I am to go, Everlasting One ! And help me to contribute to bind our glorious faith ever more with love and protection of all beautiful, innocent life. " And she repeated in German, to the milliards of Stars in space and to the great Soul of them all the sacred invocation of the European Aryans of old to our Sun : **" Heil Dir, Lichtvater alwalltende !"**

She closed her eyes for a second, as though even the vision of the glorious Sky would distract her from something invisible, after which she yearned. And suddenly it seemed to her as though the Cat was there, at her side. She heard (or thought she heard) his purr, and felt the touch of his glossy head against her face. Was the poor animal's soul the messenger of the Soul of starry Space ? Why not ?

But there was noise in the distance; it sounded as though people were gathering; a horn was heard, calling the passengers who were late. The bus was about to start.

Heliodora got up and walked back to her seat, beaming unearthly joy.

[1] Edit. 1935 p. 316.

Joda, near Barajamba, in Orissa (India).
September, 1957.
Hanover (Germany)-10th of July, 1961

———————